ŚABDA

A Study of Bhartṛhari's Philosophy of Language

ŚABDA

A Study of Bhartṛhari's Philosophy of Language

Dr. (Mrs.) Tandra Patnaik

NEW DELHI-110015

Cataloging in Publication Data — DK
Patnaik, Tandra, 1947—
Śabda : a study of Bhartṛhari's philosophy of language.
Includes bibliographical references (p.).
Includes index.

1. Bhartṛhari. Vākyapadīya. 2. Sanskrit language — Semantics. 3. Language and languages — Philosophy. I. Title.

ISBN 81-246-0028-7

First Published in India : *1994*

Published in India by:
K. Rai Mittal
Managing Director
D.K. Printworld (P) Ltd.
Regd. office : H-12, Bali Nagar
NEW DELHI - 110015
Phone : (011) 541-3463; *Fax* : (011) 559-8898

Typesetted by : Tara Chand Sons, New Delhi-110028 Ph.: 5707582

Printed at : D.K. Fine Art Press (P) Ltd., Delhi - 110052

For

Priyadarshi

Four are the definite grades of speech
The learned and wise know them
Three of these are deposited in secret
They indicate no meaning to the common man,
Men speak the fourth grade of speech
Which is phonetically expressed

***Ṛg Veda*, I.164, 45**

Foreword

THE intellectual climate for interdisciplinary research is almost non-existent in India. Under these circumstances a book on Bhartṛhari — which requires competence in philosophy, grammar as well as Sanskritic studies — is not a mean achievement. Dr Tandra Patnaik deserves special encomium for filling up a major gap in knowledge.

Present-day philosophy gives considerable attention to the distinction between the knowable and the sayable, to what is said and what is meant and to the distinction between the semantics of ordinary day-to-day discourse and the literary discourse. Dr Patnaik has assessed herself to all these questions besides giving a lucid exposition of the *Sphota* theory.

In the developmental history of philosophical thought in the West, it was only in the post-Fregean period that philosophy of language was recognised as the starting point of the study of philosophy. As Matilal points out, "The philosophy of language was a part of Indian philosophical activity from the beginning of its history." (Matilal, Bimal Krishna : *The Word and the World,* p. 4.) *Vyākaraṇa* (grammar) is one of the six *vedāṅgas* (auxiliary or preparatory disciplines for the study of *veda*). A strong and continuous grammatical tradition exists in India from the days of Pāṇini, although Pāṇini mentions several grammarians prior to him. In the West critical concern with grammar is a recent phenomenon. Whether it is Sir William Jones laying the historical foundation of the study of Indo-European, Bloomfield laying the foundation of American Structuralism, or Chomsky fathering Generative Linguistics, all have acknowledged the contribution of Pāṇini. In the field of aesthetics the Western scholars are anticipated by Indian scholars centuries ago. The theory of Crowe Ransom that poetry is language was anticipated by Rudrata's statement "*nanu śabdārtham kāvyam*" (poetry is language) and by Kunṭaka's identification of word and meaning. The Western scholars were ignorant of the rich Indian philosophical, grammatical and aesthetic traditions. The imposition of colonialism not only led them to propagate Western supremacy but also made us subservient to Western thinking.

In the chapter "The Word and the Meaning" Dr Patnaik discusses words *vs.* sentence cognition and language, ordinary meaning and what is shown but not said in language. In this presentation she succeeds in suggesting the interconnectedness between the ordinary grammatical meaning and the profound aesthetic meaning.

The present book, is a commendable introduction to India's contribution to the study of language and the interconnectedness of approaches to linguistic, philosophy, logic and aesthetics in ancient India. It is a seminal contribution to contemporary concerns of reading ancient texts in linguistics and philosophy. To the extent it is accepted by linguists and philosophers, it would have proved its merit.

Dr D. P. Pattanayak
Former Director
Central Institute of Indian Languages, Mysore

Preface

ARISTOTLE defined man as a social animal. But Bhartṛhari would have liked to define man as a 'languageing' animal. For he says: "It is the speech which prompts all mankind into activity. Without this power man is nothing more than a log of wood or a piece of stone". (*Vākyapadīya,* I. 127) In fact, the way Aristotle and Bhartṛhari define man are complementary. Man cannot live without a society; and hence society is no society without the bond of linguistic communication. Therefore language is the anchor-sheet of man's individual and social existence. This realisation has prompted the philosophers, both in the East and the West, to view 'language' as an important concept for philosophical speculation. In India, there is a rich tradition of philosophical discussion on the nature of language. But Bhartṛhari's treatise *Vākyapadīya* stands out as an unique attempt at a comprehensive philosophy of language.

The exact period during which Bhartṛhari lived is still not clear. One comes across varied estimations of the period. But on the basis of some standard evidences the time can be fixed somewhere between 450 to 500 A.D. He belonged to the Grammarian tradition of Pāṇini and Patañjali. But he transcended the limits of grammar and language analysis set by his predecessors to develop a very original philosophy of language.

Unfortunately, in the philosophical circles Bhartṛhari is a much neglected figure. He is side tracked either as a linguist or a mystic. Such contrasting pair of epithets seem quite incongruous. A linguist cannot afford to indulge in mysticism; nor can a mystic come down to the level of empirical analysis of language. Such distorted versions of Bhartṛhari's philosophical contributions prompted me to attempt an unbiased study of his work. And this made me realise that Bhartṛhari's insightful analysis of the concept of language can stand up to the challenges faced by the modern philosophers. So I decided to present this ancient philosophy of language in modern idiom — often comparing notes with the new ways of handing the issues relating to 'language'. I strongly feel that all that is a matter of antiquity need not be obsolete. Rather the present is always enriched by the wisdom of the past. As Bhartṛhari himself remarks, "the Goddess of learning does not smile on those who neglect the past." (*anupāsīta-vṛddhāṇām vidyā nāti prasīdati*) [*Vākyapadīya,* II. 493]. Besides, in philosophy we do not discover new truths with advancement of time, as it happens in case of natural sciences. In this context Jayanta Bhaṭṭa another ancient Indian philosopher offers us this crucial wisdom about doing philisophy. He says, "we cannot discover a new truth in philosophy, but we can do something novel by presenting the old truths propounded by ancients in modern terminology." (*kuto vā nūtanaṃ vastu vayaṃ utprekṣitum kṣamāḥ* | *vācovinayasavaichitrāmatraṃ atra vicārayatām.*") || [*Nyāya Mañjarī, Āhnika-1.8.*] It is no wonder, then, that the issues handled by Bhartṛhari still continue to haunt the modern philosophers. The problems are old; may be the approaches to them are new. Therefore an understanding of Bhartṛhari's philosophy may prove rewarding. Within the limited scope of this book many important dimensions of Bhartṛhari's work have been left out. I sincerely hope the new generation of scholars will take interest in them and come forward to explore them.

My fulfilment of the long cherished dream of publishing this book on Bhartṛhari could be possible because of my association with three outstanding scholars — Prof. G. Misra, Prof. B.K. Matilal and Dr. D.P. Pattanayak. My Guru Prof. G. Misra not only taught me how to do philosophy but also the difficult art of facing the challenges of life. I cannot forget the amount of enthusiasm he had shown when I started my work on Bhartṛhari. I learnt the art of presenting the ancient Indian Philosophy in contemporary idiom from reading late Prof. B.K. Matilal's works. Though I never had the opportunity of meeting him in person, he had been very prompt in answering my queries on the topic. A decade ago, Dr. D.P. Pattanayak, the then Director of Central Institute of Indian Languages, Mysore, suggested me to study Bhartṛhari. And once I started taking interest in the subject he has been constantly encouraging me to write a book on Bhartṛhari. Like a true mentor he has never allowed me to slacken the pace of my work. I pay my obeisance to these three great personalities. I salute all those great scholars like, K.A.S. Iyer, G.N. Sastri, T.R.V. Murti, H. Coward, John Brough, R.C. Pandeya and many others who have kept the interest of the scholars alive in Bhartṛhari studies through their monumental works.

My special thanks to my publishers M/s. D.K. Printworld. Their constant encouragement and constructive suggestions have provided me the necessary boost to complete the work.

Tandra Patnaik

Contents

Philosophy of Language

Its Scope and Limits

The Linguistic Turn

WHAT is language ? What is meaning? How do we communicate our thoughts through words ? How does the language function ? What is truth ? Many such 'language'-related questions have largely occupied philosopher's attention for the last few decades. Gilbert Ryle calls this phenomenon "occupational disease"[1] of twentieth century philosophy. However, it will be too much to say that philosophical activity of the century is largely confined to the narrow boundaries of 'language'-related issues. Still there is a trend of philosophy which flourishes and will continue to flourish as long as men continue to meditate on their moral nature and situation. The philosophical reflections found in the writings of Sartre, Heidegger and Nietzsche and, the latest addition to the list is surprisingly enough, Wittgenstein (latest publication *Culture and Value*) — belong to this category. What distinguishes the twentieth century philosophy from what has been done in the name of philosophy since time immemorial is the 'linguistic turn' it took in 1930s. The philosophical scene since then is dominated by those figures who prefer to call themselves 'linguistic analysts'. They claim that their avowed task is philosophical analysis of language. However, there is no unanimity in their practice of going about their job of philosophical analysis of language. So one comes across varied forms of philosophical activities under the titles of 'linguistic philosophy', 'philosophical logic' and 'philosophy of language'. It sometimes appears quite difficult to demarcate their exact area of operation.

Linguistic philosophy, primarily is the name of a method — a method of solving and dissolving the classical philosophical problems by paying attention to the ways in which certain philosophical concepts are used. Moore's analysis of the statements about the external world, Russell's analysis of definite description, Ryle's analysis of the concept of mind, Ayer's analysis of the concept of perception, etc. are some of the examples of this new way of doing philosophy. Later on, it branched off to a different way of looking at a philosopher's job, i.e., the philosopher as a therapist. He undertakes to cure intellectual disorders created by muddled use of concepts. Wittgenstein says: "The philosopher's treatment of a question is like the treatment of an illness".[2] The 'traditional' philosophers get entangled in problems when they allow the concepts to 'idle' and get detached from their actual use. So "what **we** do is to bring words back from their metaphysical to their everyday use",[3] says Wittgenstein summing up the nature of the therapy.

Philosophical logic, on the other hand, is not the name of a method but a special approach to philosophical understanding. Broadly speaking, it "considers the vocabulary of logic. What constitutes a statement, in what 'logical form' consists or implication or entailment or disjunction or modality...".[4] It aims at finding out the 'logic' of propositions, of truth, of reference, of predication. Wittgenstein of *Tractatus Logico Philosophicus*, Russell, Frege, Strawson, Grice, all the adherents of philosophical logic try to explicate the logical structure of language and the issues related to proposition, truth, reference, etc. in their own ways. Russell even goes to the extent of saying that philosophical logic **is** the philosophy. However, in later phases, this approach was extended to unfold the 'logic of morality', the 'logic of religion', the 'logic of justice', etc. The most important example of this specialized version of philosophical logic is R.M. Hare's analysis of the nature of most general moral concepts to demarcate the structure of moral argument and moral assertions.

Philosophy of language, is considered to be distinct from philosophical logic in the sense that it does not aim at providing a structural geography of any and every concept. Philosophy of language, as the name suggests exclusively deals with the basic principles of 'language' and the concepts associated with the general forms of language. In a certain sense, it does not appear to be very different from the strict and original version of philosophical logic. According to Searle — one of the chief exponents of philosophy of language, it aims "to give philosophically illuminating description of certain general features of language".[5] Philosophy of language proposes to deal with issues such as meaning, truth, reference, necessity, etc. Searle also clearly indicates that philosophy of language should not be confused with linguistics. According to him "linguistics attempts to describe the actual structures — phonological, syntactical and semantic — of natural human languages".[6] Though philosophy of language draws its data from natural human languages, yet its theories and conclusions are supposed to be true of any **possible** language. Philosophy of language in short, deals with **language**, not **languages**.

However, the development of thoughts during the last two decades shows that the boundaries between linguistic philosophy, philosophical logic, philosophy of language and linguistics are gradually becoming fluid. Linguistic philosophy as a method of conceptual analysis is not opposed to the rest. One can apply the method of linguistic analysis while doing philosophical logic or philosophy of language. But the areas of philosophy of language, linguistics and philosophical logic mostly criss-cross each other. J.J. Passmore while assessing the post-Wittgensteinian developments in his book *Recent Philosophers* observes that, "Philosophical logic fades into philosophy of language and that....into linguistics".[7] The present science of linguistics, especially the Chomskian model of understanding it, incorporates within its scope much of what was counted as philosophy of language. Therefore, in the present context with overlapping of boundaries amongst specialised areas of study of language one can broadly say that philosophy of language stands for understanding the structural principles of "how language functions".

The Indian Viewpoint

In case of Indian philosophical developments we notice that the inquisitiveness about 'language' as a concept is as old as Indian culture itself. By saying so, I don't claim that in Western thought the concept of language and meaning was not discussed at all prior to the twentieth century 'linguistic turn'. Plato made significant contributions to the analysis of 'meaning' through his theory of 'Ideas'. But subsequently it never drew that much of attention. J.F. Staal while writing on "Sanskrit Philosophy of Language" very aptly observes : "at times almost excessive preoccupation with language on the one hand and with philosophy on the other, may indeed be regarded as a characteristic of Indian Civilization".[8] The comment is justified in the sense that *Ṛg Veda,* one of the oldest scriptures of India, contains innumerable insightful remarks about the nature of language (*śabda*) and Speech (*vāk*). The subsequent scriptures and texts are full of elaborate discussions on the concept of language and its purpose. Of course, the nature of the discussion is largely determined by the cultural and philosophical tradition of the time. We must be fully aware of the fact that such deliberations occur several centuries back in time. At the same time, the area of discourse and the scope of discussion has many things common with the modern version of the philosophy of language. The varied philosophical systems that flourished in ancient India concentrate on certain common themes, such as, the problem of meaning, word-world relationship, speaker-hearer relationship, the formal conditions of language and communicability, etc.

Most of the philosophical systems of India take up the problem of language as a part of their epistemological concern, otherwise known as *pramāṇa śāstra.* As is well-known, they draw a clear line of distinction between *jñāna* (roughly translated, it means 'cognition') and *pramā* (knowledge). While analysing the concept of *pramā* they categorise different methods or means of knowledge (*pramāṇa*). However, there is no unanimity of views regarding the number of such valid methods of knowledge. Some like *Purvamīmāṁsā* and *Vedānta,* admit of six methods — *Pratyakṣa.* (perception), *Anumāna* (inference), *Upamāna* (comparison), *Arthāpatti* (postulation), *Anupalabdhi* (non-apprehension) and *Śabda* (verbality); whereas Cārvāka accepts only the method of *pratyakṣa* as valid. So it is obvious that all the schools of thought do not accord independent status to *śabda* as a *pramāṇa. Nyāya, Mīmāṁsā, Vedānta, Sāṅkhya* are such systems which admit the validity of *śabda pramāṇa* and carry on elaborate discussions on the nature of language and its functions. In this connection it may be noted that though Buddhism does not offer the status of independent *pramāṇa* to *śabda*, a very powerful analysis of the concept of language and meaning is found in Buddhistic literature. The *apoha* theory of meaning, advocated by Buddhist logicians Diṇṇāga and Dharmakīrti, is unique and novel in many respects. I intend to refer to this theory in a separate chapter.

Does *Śabda Pramāṇa* mean Scriptural Authority ?

Śabda pramāṇa, broadly translated means the linguistic method of obtaining knowledge (both, oral and written); and is distinctively different from the other methods of knowledge. Unlike, the methods of perception, inference, etc., facts and sense-objects do not form the basis of such knowledge. As a linguistic means of knowledge its object is language itself. However, the traditional interpretation found in innumerable English books on the subject leaves us with the impression that it means nothing more than knowledge based on some form of 'authority'. The term *śabda pramāṇa* is very often translated as "verbal authority", which tends to shift the emphasis from the linguistic aspect to the 'authoritative' aspect of the theory. Of course, these interpreters have their own justification because some of the definitions confirm their views. But here it seems to be a case of going by the letter than the spirit of what has been discussed within the scope of *śabda pramāṇa*. To justify this point we need to examine very briefly what the different schools of Indian philosophy state about *śabda pramāṇa*.

Gotama, the founder of *Nyāya* School of thought defines *Śabda* as *āptopadeśa śabdaḥ* (*Nyāya Sūtras*, 1.1.7) — "the assertion or instruction of a trustworthy person is *Śabda*". The term *āpta* applies to both 'a reliable' human being and God, because *Nyāya* believes that God is the creator of *Vedas* (the highest form of scripture). Regarding the qualities of an human *āpta*, Vātsyāyana specifies the following qualities: "He (who) has realised or perceived the *dharma*, he is engaged in making a statement in order to communicate objects or facts as he has perceived them".[9] However, *Nyāya* offers higher status to the instructions and assertions of *Veda*, for they are unquestionably and unconditionally true. Such words concerning *dharma* (moral conduct) are the words of God, hence authentic and uncontradictable. Even regarding the nature of human *āpta*, some interpreters[10] argue that by *āpta* Vātsyāyana means not an ordinary person but a seer-teacher (*ṛṣi*), hence his assertions are beyond doubt. Like *Nyāya*, *Mīmāṁsā* talks of two types of linguistic sources — *laukika* (human) and *vaidika* (*Vedic* or scriptural). But Kumārila, one of its exponents holds a different view. He accords the status of *śabda pramāṇa* only to *Vedic* instructions. Even Prabhākara, another important *Mīmāṁsaka*, who initially accepts *āpta vākya* as authentic, later on reduces it to *anumāna* (inference), for the validity of such assertions are inferred from the trustworthiness of the speaker. One noteworthy feature of *Mīmāṁsā* view of *śabda* is that it accords a special status to the *Karmakāṇḍa* portion of the *Vedas* which is full of injunctive statements about sacrifices, rites and moral behaviour of man. For them *Vedic* statements are injunctive, not informative in nature. *Sāṁkhya* philosophers, on the other hand, hold a slightly different view about *śabda pramāṇa*. For them *vedic* statements are the only statements which are free from all sorts of doubt, hence self-valid. But their self-validity is due to the non-personal authorship of *Vedas*. The *vedic* words have a natural power to denote worldly objects and that power is communicated by *āptas*. "Hence the self-validity of *Vedas* are tested and lived by the *āptas*".[11] *Advaita Vedānta*, offers primacy to *śabda* as a *pramāṇa* because it is a means of acquiring philosophical knowledge (*pāramārthika tattva-bhedakatā*) and not empirical knowledge (*vyāvahārika*) which is acquired by means of perception, inference, etc. It also offers higher status to *veda vākyas*. But here *veda vākyas* do not refer to what is contained in *Karmakāṇḍa*, but only the *Vedānta* portions, which contain statements about the nature of the highest Reality. Śaṅkara while emphasising the importance of scriptural assertions says: "The means (in fact, knowledge-how) that can be known neither by perception nor by inference is what they come through scriptures. And this constitutes the scripturehood of the scriptures".[12] Here by *Śruti* or the text of *Vedas* he specifically refers to *mahāvākyas* (great assertions) like *tat tvam asi*, (that thou art), etc. They lead us to the ultimate form of knowledge that frees us from wordly expectations and desires and forms the basis of our knowledge of the ultimate Reality (*Brahma jñāna*).

From the above way of presentation of the concept of *śabda pramāṇa* one may gather the impression that the Indian tradition encourages blind and dogmatic acceptance of scriptural assertions.

In spite of this, surprisingly enough, we find no clear indication about 'authority' as a source of knowledge in the sense the term is understood by medieval Western philosophers. Rather the *Veda* is called *apauruṣeya* (non-personal and authorless). Therefore, there is plenty of scope for confusion if the terms *śabda pramāṇa* and *āgama* are translated as verbal 'authority' and scriptural 'authority' respectively. But it seems, some Indian writers in English have strong fascination for the term 'authority'. This is because still some 'so-called' traditionalists believe that the *Vedic* statements are to be accepted unquestionably and unconditionally. Hence 'authority' is the favoured term.

Dayakrishna rightly remarks "The notion of *Vedic* authority is ...a myth''.[13] Yet a large number of thinkers do not want the 'myth' to be exploded. To silence them we have put some counter questions. By this process we can set the record straight. So let us start with the question about the exact significance of the term 'scriptural authority'. If it means the unquestioning acceptance of *Vedic* assertions (without any scope for analysis and interpretation of their true meaning) then the traditionalists have wrongly assessed the Indian tradition. Interpretability is very much a part of it. So within ancient texts and commentaries we notice varied and sometimes contrary interpretations of the same *Vedic* stanzas and lines. Bhartṛhari in his *Vākyapadīya* offers us the finest examples of such variations in interpretation of meanings. He says: "Based on explanatory comments and similar passages, conflicting views have been set forth by the exponents of Monism and Dualism".[14] In his commentary following the verse he goes on to elaborate the point further: "Because of the diversity of human intellect, diversity of specualtions take place''. He cites several examples to illustrate his point. I take one such example to prove his point. The famous *Upaniṣadic* verse — "Two birds, companions, united together, occupy the same tree. Of the two one eats the tasty fig fruit, while the other does not eat, only shines" — has been interpreted in different manners. To the Monist, "By two 'birds' the senses and the inner controller, the intelligence or the soul is meant". The Dualists on the other hand, interprete 'two birds' as "the differentiated and the undifferentiated consciousness full of seeds". Those who advocate that *Vedic* statements signify 'authority', and hence its truth and meaning is unquestionable, gloss over such explanations found within the Indian traditional texts. In fact, the idea of interpretability is as old as Indian culture itself. Yāska, one of the ancient etymologists (700 B.C.) highlights this aspect when he says that without the interpretation of meaning *Vedic* statements are like "barren cow and mere illusion" (*adhenumāyā*).[15] The importance of interpretation in Indian tradition is evident from the fact that innumerable philosophical views flourished here, in spite of each claiming to follow the *Vedic* lineage. Their views varied widely because they offered different inerpretations of *Vedic* passages or most often focused attention on this or that aspect of *Vedas* which suited their own metaphysical model. If we come to the specific texts the line of argument may become more clear. *Brahma Sūtra* is regarded as a part of the *Śruti* by *Vedāntins.* But Śaṅkara and Rāmānuja offer quite different versions of the same text.[16] If *Vedic* statements and *Śruti* would have been considered to be the embodiment of final truth this freedom of interpretation would not have been there. These facts justify that the choice of the term 'authority' is a wrong one or else a myth that the traditionalists want to perpetuate at any cost.

The next question that I want to raise about the identification of *śabda-pramāṇa* with 'verbal authority' is still more crucial. If *śabda-pramāṇa* means acquisition of knowledge by blindly accepting what the scriptures say, then why do the Indian Philosophers waste so much of time and energy in analysing different dimensions of the concept of 'language'? Indian philosophical literature is full of very rich and penetrating discussions about the nature of language, meaning, word-world relationship, speaker-hearer relationship and many more language-related issues. Many logical issues are raised within the scope of such discussions. These philosophers, who exhibit rare analytical acumen in their treatment of the concept of language could not have been so dumb as to advocate dogmatic acceptance of the 'authority' of scriptures. The traditionalists, may put some quotations in support of their stand. But this does not provide much strength to their argument. There are plenty of statements and definitions found within the same texts, which are enough to challenge their viewpoint. Let me illustrate this with some statements and definitions found in different texts about the nature of *śabda pramāṇa* and *śruti. Sāṁkhya* defines *Śruti* as "knowledge obtained by analysis of meaning" (*vākya janitam vākyārtha jñānam śruti*). Similarly Śaṇkara puts emphasis on the analysis of meaning (*vākyārtha vicāraṇā*) even in case of the highest form of knowledge (*Brahma jñāna*). He says: "Comprehension of *Brahman* is affected by the ascertainment, consequent on discussion, of the meaning of *Vedānta* statements".[17] This, to a large extent, disproves the traditionalists argument that *Brahma jñāna* is a matter of mystical experience only, and has nothing to do with language analysis. Similary, according to *Sāṁkhya, Vedic* statements are not anybody's assertions, but have a natural power to denote, which are communicated to common man by *āptas* only. So *āptas* become the medium for the acquisition of scriptural knowledge. But any and every interpretation offered by *āptas* are not to be accepted dogmatically. In this context Aniruddha in his *vṛtti* on Vācaspati's *Tattva Kaumudī* says: "Huge giants do not drop from heaven simply because an *āpta*, or competent person says so. Only sayings which are **supported by reason** should be accepted by me and others like yourselves".[18] Again, Bhartṛhari very rightly points out that there is always the possibility of doubt in case of verbal authority because the intended meaning may not be correctly grasped by the hearer. There are many such instances[19] where the emphasis is put on understanding of the correct meaning by language analysis and the application of reason. The 'so-called' traditionalists only present one side of the story without giving the other side any chance. On their procrustean bed they chop-off everything that does not conform to their interpretation.

Still, the upholders of 'authority' of scriptures may be left with some more arguments in their favour. It may be argued that the scriptural assertions imply unquestioning acceptance because they are supposed to be uncontradictable and incorrigible. This type of knowledge is only assured by *śabda pramāṇa*. This is admitted by most of the schools of classical Indian systems. But such characterisations should not be understood at the surface level only. They have deeper significance. The uncontradictability and incorrigibility of scriptural assertions are due to the nature of these statements. According to *Mīmāṁsakas* the *Vedic* statements are injunctive in nature and they do not inform us about facts. They are concerning commands (*vidhi*) and prohibitions (*niśedha*). Such statements cannot be challenged, because such **prescriptive** rules cannot be negated, once accepted. Similarly, according to *Nyāya Vedic* statements are concerning *dharma* (which in broader Indian context means moral principles). Moral principles too are prescriptive by nature, hence uncontradictable. On the other hand, for *Vedāntins* (especially *Advaitins*) scriptural statements are non-empirical and philosophical by nature (*pāramārthika tattva*), so they cannot be contradicted by factual knowledge. They make a clear distinction between **factual** (*vyāvahārika*) and **philosophical** (*pāramārthika*) statements. Factual statement can contradict a factual statement, not a non-factual statement. That is why Vācaspati says: "even a thousand scriptures cannot turn the knowledge of pot into the knowledge of cloth".[20] In other words, the ways and means of acquiring factual knowledge are different from the knowledge acquired through linguistic means and scriptures. Scriptural statements have nothing to do with facts. Factual knowledge cannot contradict or correct the non-factual knowledge. So it seems that there is no mystery surrounding the scriptural knowledge. I do not at the same time deny the fact that there are many such verses and statements in philosophical texts of different systems which openly declare loyalty to *Vedic* words. But beyond this apparent dogmatism there lies mines of ideas which are highly logical and analytical in nature. We cannot afford to neglect them while understanding the concept of *śabda pramāṇa*.

Bhartṛhari: The New Way of Looking at Language

Let us now take up for consideration a completely new way of handling the concept of language or *śabda*. This is embodied in Bhartṛhari's treatise entitled *Vākyapadīya*. As the title suggests, it should have been on 'words' and 'sentences'; instead it expounds a ful-fledged philosophy of language. This is evident from the outline Bhartṛhari himself offers about the scope of the subject-matter of his treatise. He specifies eight topics coming within the fold of his study. They are : (1) meaning determined through analysis (abstracted meaning), (2) given or stable meaning conveyed through the sentence, (3) linguistic forms that figure in grammatical derivations, (4) linguistic forms that are to be analysed, (5) cause-effect relationship between the intention of the speaker and the utterance, (6) the relationship of capability between the forms of speech and the meaning, (7) the relations that lead to merit, (8) the relations that bring out communication.[21] All these topics mentioned above do not come exclusively within the ambit of 'grammar' (as understood in the ordinary sense). The list of topics clearly indicates that Bhartṛhari's interest is not confined to the rules and forms of language. Rather he aims at a depth-analysis of the concepts of language and meaning. We have every reason to believe that Bhartṛhari's *Vākyapadīya* is a comprehensive treatise on philosophy of language.

However, it seems that in ancient India a clear line of distinction was maintained between *Dārśanikas* (technically speaking, philosophers) and *Vaiyākaraṇikas* (the Grammarians). So Bhartṛhari the Grammarian's trespassing into the area of philosophy was neither welcomed by *Dārśanikas* nor *Vaiyākaraṇikas.* Somānanda and Utpalācārya, the later Grammarians, comment that as a Grammarian, Bhartṛhari should have confined himself to the business of explaining the forms of sanskrit language instead of making an effort to dabble in metaphysics and epistemology.[22] But in spite of such distinction between philosophy and grammar one finds that Bhartṛhari's theories of *Śabda Brahman, sphoṭa, pratibhā,* etc., are taken up for discussion by almost all the schools of Indian Philosophy. Right from Śaṅkara to Diṇṇāga, most of the philosophers refer to his theory (either directly mentioning his name or indirectly). Most often they repudiate his views. But if his theory would be lacking in philosophical contents, there would have been no necessity of even repudiating it. Still, it is a fact that Bhartṛhari has not been offered the status he deserved, either by the classical philosophers or by the modern philosophers.

Bhartṛhari in his *magnum opus Vākyapadīya* (a treatise with three *Kāṇḍas*) treats the concept of *śabda* as the ultimate concern for his philosophical exploration. He also discusses *śabda* as a *pramāṇa*, like other classical philosophical systems. Since in the last section I have focused on the concept of *śabda* as a *pramāṇa*, it would be relevant for us to understand how Bhartṛhari views the issue, and to assess whether in any way he falls short of the philosophical standards reached by *Dārśanikas.* Bhartṛhari accepts *pratyakṣa, anumāna* and *śabda* as the relevant methods of valid knowledge. But in his opinion all these methods are not full-proof. One can get a glimpse of his analytical acumen from the way he proves the unreliability of these methods. He observes that perception is helpful as a means of factual knowledge. But perception as a method has limitations. For sense perceptions can be deceptive. He argues: "The sky looks like a solid surface and fire-fly like a spark (of fire), (but we know that it is all wrong) for there is no solid surface and no fire in the fire-fly".[23] Similarly *anumāna* is useful as an aid to perception. Yet when we can commit errors in case of perception, what to speak of the inference which is indirect in nature? Similar is the case with *āpta vākyas*, i.e., verbal knowledge acquired through the assertions of trustworthy persons. Bhartṛhari points out, "What one acquires from other people's words may be coloured by one's background".[24] It can sometimes be sensibly different from what the speaker intended to say. Even *Vedic* statements can have varying interpretations depending upon the metaphysical position one adopts. So what according to him is the right method of obtaining incorrigible knowledge ? Bhartṛhari's answer sounds interesting. He says that "we cannot understand the meaning of the words of *āgama* by merely hearing them, we have to use reasoning to determine the meaning and this does not amount to going against the *Vedas.*[25] This power of understanding the meaning is due to the inherent power, *pratibhā* (intuition) and *śabda bhāvanā* (linguistic potency) present within us. He elaborates different ways and phases through which this power can be realised. But for the time being we shall not go into details, because our concern here is not exactly epistemological analysis, but the philosophy of language that Bhartṛhari presents.

It is interesting to note that the term *śabda pramāṇa* acquires a new dimension in the philosophy of Grammar. Bhartṛhari derives his philosophical inspiration from Patañjali's *Mahābhāṣya.* Patañjali identifies himself as *śabda pramānaka.* Here the term *śabda pramāṇaka* cannot be translated as, "the follower of scriptural authority". The term has a broader connotation, as is evident from the contexts in which Patañjali uses the term. He says "*śabda pramāṇaka vayam yacchabda āha tad asmākam pramāṇam*". With reference to the context[26] the above line should be translated in the following manner — "We are the analysist of language, for us, what the word presents is our only way of knowing". In other words he claims that as a *śabda pramāṇakas* his job is to understand facts and objects through linguistic forms only. Commenting on Patañjali's statement Bhartṛhari says : "*kim asmākam vastugatena vicāreṇa ? arthastvasmākaṃ yaḥ śabdenābhidhīyate*".[27] This means, "what is the use of our reflecting on the nature of things ? The object for us is what the word presents". This statement should be taken as the basic presupposition of Bhartṛhari's approach to philosophical exploration. For him the limit of language is the limit of the reality. This novel approach to the subject-matter of philosophy results in a unique philosophy of language. This also makes his position different from other grammarians as well as philosophers of India.

Bhartṛhari's way of unfolding 'what the words present' is both insightful and philosophically illuminating. He understands the world in terms of words. The nature of objects and existence in the world, according to him, is determined by how we cognise it. How we cognise it, in turn, is determined by word-impregnated concepts. Without the use of linguistic elements concepts cannot be formed. Therefore, as a conclusion, it follows that objects, their cognition and linguistic expressions about the affairs of the world — all of them, are dependent on the one and unitary linguistic principle (*śabda tattva*). In fact, he studies the concept of language at two levels — (1) language viewed as an **act**, and (2) language viewed as a **principle** (*tattva*). At the level of act, language functions as a communicative tool. So he undertakes an elaborate analysis of the elements involved in the act of linguistic communication. Again, at the transcendental level, the concept of 'language' serves as a metaphysical principle, through which he attempts to explain the phenomenal world. Thus 'language' (*śabda*) acquires the status of the highest Reality, i.e., the *śabda Brahman*.

Bhartṛhari's concern with *śabda* has many areas common with what has been discussed by classical Indian systems within the scope of *śabda-pramāṇa*. All of them analyse the nature of language and meaning, world-word relationship, the primacy of either the word-meaning or the sentence-meaning, and the different dimensions of meaning. But Bhartṛhari's method of approaching 'language' is different from others. Bhartṛhari presents the entire gamut of human understanding by analysing the structural conditions of language. His job is not only confined to the analysis of language but also to work out the boundaries of what we can do and cannot do with language.

Metaphysics and Language

If by 'philosophy of language' we mean "offering philosophically illuminating description of general features of language", then most of what the Indian philosophers along with Bhartṛhari discuss comes within its scope. But if by philosophy of language we mean understanding the complex phenomena of how we communicate our thoughts through language, and laying bare the structure of 'how language functions'; then Bhartṛhari's way of handling the problem comes closest to this objective. Matilal very rightly observes: "The overall concern with how our language works was not the chief concern of most classical Indian philosophers, except for the grammarians like Bhartṛhari".[28] But it is obvious that Bhartṛhari's concern goes beyond just explicating the structural principles of 'how language works'. He wants to present a comprehensive picture of epistemology, metaphysics and linguistics through his conception of *Śabda tattva.* So in certain respects his aim and objective is different from that of other philosophers of language, past and present. Rather, Bhartṛhari's way of handling philosophy of language in certain respects can be described as a form of **metaphysics** of language because he proposes to connect all dimensions of philosophical activity through the network of linguistic and conceptual forms. In this respect Bhartṛhari's model of metaphysics is akin to what Strawson identifies as the 'connective' model of philosophical analysis. It is a matter of interesting co-incidence that Strawson elucidates the model with the analogy of grammar (as opposed the analogy of 'therapy' offered by Wittgenstein). According to him, "just as the grammarian. . .labours to produce a systematic account of the structure of rules which we effortlessly observe in speaking grammatically, so the philosopher labours to produce a systematic account of the general **conceptual structure** of which our daily practice shows us to have a tacit and unconscious mastery".[29] With the introduction of this model Strawson proposes to show the interconnection between the irreducible notions which form the basic structure of our thinking; through which ontology, epistemology and logic can be seen as the three aspects of one unified inquiry. Bhartṛhari's method of analysis as well as the objective of his analysis is closer to the above-mentioned model because he lays bare the structural elements of language of which the language user has tacit understanding but no explicit knowledge. And with these structural elements he develops a unified scheme of philosophical inquiry. But, we can go thus far with our comparison, no further. Strawson's approach to metaphysics is 'descriptive' — he understands the basic and irreducible concepts in terms of our actual operation with language and concepts. It does not aim at providing a revised picture of the "structure of our thought about the world", by pushing one concept in favour of the other. Strawson is very much aware of this risk in case of pursuing the 'connective' model of philosophical analysis. He warns: "There is, as it were, a tendency to intellectual imperialism. . ."[30] Philosophers have a tendency to produce a strikingly different world-picture dominated by a particular concept, representing a particular attitude and interest. Most of the philosophers would not like to leave their philosophical inquiry half-way without a final conceptual committment. In case of Bhartṛhari, his philosophical inquiry about the nature of language culminates in the idea of *śabda Brahman.* It is a form of Monism in which the principle of language is identified with the Reality; otherwise known as *śabdādvaitavāda* (Linguistic Monism). Some Modern thinkers, like Matilal, are of opinion that Bhartṛhari was one of the earliest exponents of *Advaita* — (the philosophy of non-dualism) a form of Monism made popular by Śaṅkara.

One of the unique features of Bhartṛhari's philosophical inquiry is that he starts with the concept one *śabda Brahman* as the ground of all phenomenal multiplicities and changes. Then he goes on to unravel the structural concepts of language and thought and ends his inquiry with an analysis of the nature of utterances. In this sense his treatise *Vākyapadīya,* constituted of three parts, is a complete book in the area of language analysis.

Metaphysics and Mysticism

Before concluding this Introductory chapter I intend to make certain issues clear. First of all, we should not have any qualms about the metaphysical nature of Bhartṛhari's work. It will be a distortion of truth to say that his metaphysics is a superficial part of his philosophical inquiry about language. He was part of a tradition — a tradition in which every form of intellectual activity is directed towards the realisation of the ultimate knowledge. Be it poetics, music or grammar — every form of inquiry aims to explain the phenomenal in terms of transcendental. It is not a case of deification of concepts but a search for perfection symbolized in the concept of Reality. So Bhartṛhari's philosophy of Linguistic Monism is the culmination of his intellectual inquiry conforming to the trends of the Indian culture and tradition. But in no sense can it be called "unscientific" and "poetic"[31] as W.T. Stace very crudely remarks about the Indian tradition in general, in his book *A Critical History of Greek Philosophy.* Metaphysics, in the sense of

'Speculative' Metaphysics, is not so peculiar to Indian tradition. The obsession with the concept of "Highest Reality" was very dominant in Western thought, too. Ironically enough, Stace makes such a comment in the **Introduction** of a book in which he discusses the philosophy of Plato, who was famous for his use of poetic metaphors and myths in philosophy. Perhaps he was guided by the dogmatic belief that "Indian thought is usually excluded from the history of philosophy because. . . .it lies outside the mainstream of human development''.[32] I strongly feel, that if one wants to do philosophy or write on philosophy, he should not have a closed mind. By this I also refer to some Indian Scholars who try to put Indian Philosophical views in the straight-jacket of Western thought. Ancient philosophers can be understood in modern idiom, without stripping them off their cultural and traditional wrappings. In this book I have attempted to stick to this way of presentation.

Another strong bias is specifically floated about Bhartṛhari. It is believed that Bhartṛhari is a linguist. Hence philosophers have nothing to do with him. The bias has its roots in ancient distinction between *Dārśanikas* and *Vaiyākaraṇikas*. It seems, that modern Indian scholars are still under the spell of a very ancient (but now obsolete) dogma. This is evident from the fact that volumes are written on the nature of language analysis undertaken by the accredited Indian classical philosophical systems, but not on Bhartṛhari. It is left to scholars on Sanskrit to keep the philosophical views of Bhartṛhari alive. I feel that the modern scholars must throw away such a bias in view of the recent developments of thought, when the demarcating line between linguistics and philosophy of language is getting blurred.

References

1. Gilbert Ryle, *Collected Papers*, II, London : Hutchinson and Co. Ltd., 1973, p. 150.
2. L. Wittgenstein, *Philosophical Investigations*, London: Basil and Blackwell, 1978, p. 255.
3. *Ibid.* p. 116.

4. John Passmore, *Recent Philosophers : A Supplement to Hundred Years of Philosophy,* London: Duckworth, 1985, p. 6.
5. John Searle, *Speech-Acts : An Essay in the Philosophy of Language,* Cambridge : Cambridge University Press, 1969, p. 2.
6. *Ibid.*
7. Passmore, *Recent Philosophers,* p. 6.
8. B.K. Matilal, *The Word and the World,* Delhi: Oxford University Press, 1990, p. 5.
9. *Ibid.*, p. 6.
10. J.V. Bhattacharya, *Nyāya Mañjarī of Jayanta Bhaṭṭa,* Delhi : Motilal Banarsidass, 1965 p. 316.
11. *Sāṁkhya Pravacana Bhāṣya,* V. 43, as translated by S. Radhakrishnan, *Indian Philosophy,* Vol. 1, London : Goerge Allen and Unwin, 1962, p. 301.
12. Śaṅkara under *Brahma Sūtra,* 2.1.1.

    pratyakṣenānumityā va yastūpāyo no budhyate
    enam vidhanti vedana tasmād vedasya vedatā ||

13. Dayakrishna, "Three Myths about Indian Philosophy", In *Indian Philosophy : A Counter Perspective,* Delhi : Oxford University Press, 1991, p. 9.

    See this book for more arguments against the 'myth' of Authority and other associated myths that are responsible for a distorted presentation of Indian Philosophy.

14. *Vākyapadīya,* 1.8. tr. by K.A.S. Iyer, Poona : Deccan College, 1965.
15. Yāska, *Nirukta,* 1.20. Quoted from *The Cultural Heritage of India,* Vol.I, Caltutta: The Ramakrishna Mission, 1982, p. 293.
16. *Bṛhadāraṇyaka Upaniṣad,* 4.3.12 says that while dreaming the 'immortal' freely moves about, leaving its nest. While commenting upon this Śaṅkara says: It is 'impossible to speak of an animal that sleeps, that it runs and comes back from a place where it sleeps from by thousand and thousand of miles. So this does not stand to reason. It is stated elsewhere in the same text that the dreamer moves inside the body only. So Śaṅkara's conclusion is that *śrutis* such as these are to be explained away as merely figurative speech. *Brahma Sūtra Śaṅkara Bhāṣya,* 3.2.3.
17. *Brahma Sūtra Bhāṣya* of Śaṅkara, 1.1.2:

    vākyārtha vicāraṇādhyavaṣānanivṛttahi brahmāvagatiḥ
    nānumānadi pramānāntara nivṛtta.

18. *nāhy āpta vacānān nabhaso nipatanti mahāsurāḥ,*
yuktimad vacanam grāhyam mayānaica bhavadvidhaiḥ.
Quoted from Radhakrishnan's *Indian Philosophy*, p. 802.

19. "Logical analysis must aid interpretation of scriptures" (*Śrutyaivaca sahavatvena tarkasyāpy' bhyupetatvat*) *Śaṅkara* under *Brahma Sūtra Bhāṣya*, 1.1.2.

Professor G. Misra pioneered the movement of interpreting *Advaita* Concept of *Śabda Pramāṇa* as a method of Logico-Linguistic method. For his interpretation *see* his *Advaita Philosophy : Its Method, Scope and Limits* (Bhubaneswar : 1976). Also refer the *The Proceedings of Fifth Conference of All Orissa Philosophy Association* (Bhubaneswar, Post-Graduate Department of Philosophy, 1973) for a critical discussion on *Śabda Pramāṇa* under the symposium on the topic. In a paper included in the volume. J.Dash makes a very interesting point regarding Śaṅkara's method; "Acharya's method seems to start with authorities and then, in final analysis, to discard them, even as costly lunar model by the Lunarnauts".

20. *Na hy āgamah sahasrā nāni ghaṭam pratyitamsate* (*Bhamati* Introduction.)

Śaṅkara says: "validity of a statement about observable attributes of an object may be done by help of sense-perception, etc., statements about objects which cannot be verified by empirical means must be done by language analysis".

Śaṅkara Bhāṣya on *Bhagavad Gītā*, 18.66.

21. *Vākyapadīya*, I. 24-26. As summarised by A. Akjulkar and K. Potter in *Encyclopaedia of Indian Philosophies*, Vol. V. (*The Philosophy of Grammarians*), ed. by H.G. Coward and K.K. Raja., Delhi, Motilal Banarsidass, 1990, pp. 129-30.

22. K.A. Subramania Iyer, *Bhartṛhari*, Poona : Deccan College, 1969, p. 70.

23. *Talavad dṛśyate vyoma khadyotoivyavādiva* ।
Naiva nāsti talam vyomni na khadyoto hutāsanaḥ ॥ (*Vāk.*, II, 140)

24. *Vaktrānyathaiva prakrānto bhinneṣu pratipattṛṣu* ।
Svapratyānukāreṇa śabdārtha pravibhājyate ॥ (*Vāk.* II, 135)

25. *Vedaśāstra virodhi ca tarkasacakṣur paśyatam* ।
Rūpamātrādi vākyārtha kevalannāvatiṣṭhate ॥ (*Vāk.* I. 127, 135).

26. *Mahābhāṣya* pt. II.1.1. What the word says is our authority. And the words say here that "something is — this" (is a stick); 'is' is implied. That stick which is agent, when combined with another word, (becomes instrument).

27. Bhartṛhari, *Mahābhāṣya Dipikā*, Part I, Poona, Bhandarkar Oriental Research Institute, 1967, p. 28.1. 16-18.

28. Matilal, *The word and the World,* p. 4.
29. P.F. Strawson, *Analysis and Metaphysics,* Oxford: Oxford University Press, 1992, p.5.
30. *Ibid.*, p. 14.
31. W.T. Stace, *A Critical History of Greek Philosophy,* Delhi: Macmillan and Co., Ltd., 1982, p. 16.
32. *Ibid.*

2

Śabdādvaitavāda
The Metaphysics of Language

Śabda Brahman: Its Implications

BHARTṚHARI starts his philosophical exploration with the concept of *śabda Brahman*. This, according to him, is the unique and ultimate Reality. The concepts of existence, consciousness and language-in-use, which are associated with our understanding of the empirical world exhibit the elements of plurality. Yet all these concepts are word-generated. So they are bound by a common essence. And this essence is called by Bhartṛhari *śabda tattva*, the **language-principle.** It is the ultimate principle of unity, hence the ultimate reality, the *Brahman*. It is obvious that Bhartṛhari offers primacy to the concept of 'unity' in his metaphysical scheme. Therefore, *śabda Brahman* signifies supreme unity rather than supreme existence. All along his attempt has been to show how the pluralities of the phenomenal world direct us towards an ultimate form of unity. To understand Bhartṛhari's metaphysics, therefore, we will have to assess how far he has been successful in explaining plurality in terms of unity.

The opening verse of his treatise *Vākyapadīya* epitomises his metaphysical approach. It says:

> *anādinidhānaṁ bra śabdatattvaṁ yadakṣaraṁ* |
> *vivartate arthabhāvena prakriyā jagato yataḥ* ||

Following K.A.S. Iyer we can translate the verse as follows:

> The *Brahman* is without beginning and end, whose essence is the Word, who is the cause of the manifested phonemes, who appears as the objects, from whom the creation of the world proceeds.[1]

Literally understood the statement may appear to be a sort of mystical rhapsody. For, how can the objects and the world proceed from the Word ? So the entire idea seems uncritical and non-philosophical. But the above verse has a deeper significance which gradually unfolds as Bhartṛhari proceeds with his task in *Vākyapadīya*. Here, I shall make an attempt to unravel the significance of the verse by examining the imports of terms and phrases contained in it. This may provide us enough ground for assessing how much of it is mystical and how much is logical.

The first concept that needs elucidation is *śabda*. Very broadly understood it means sound. If we go for a stricter interpretation then *śabda* means "uttered or written strings of words having a syntax and meaning". In short, it means 'language'. This is the sense in which the term has been used in case of *śabda pramāṇa* by other philosophical systems. But for Bhartṛhari *śabda* means something more than 'language'. It is the name of a complex phenomenon implying an activity as well as a principle. As a type of activity it is something in which all human beings, in fact, all sentient beings are engaged. The Sanskrit term for it is *śabdanā vyāpāra*. B.K. Matilal translates it as 'languageing'.[2] Again as a principle it stands for the very potency for communicating thoughts through language. It is the linguistic potency, the very power of conceptualisation, which is the basis of our consciousness as well as the awareness of the external world. This potency itself is *śabda tattva*, the **word principle.** The *śabda tattva*, being the central concept of all forms of phenomenal activity is identified with the *Brahman*. The term *Brahman* in *Advaitin* and *Upaniṣadic* context means the 'Reality', in a metaphysical sense. But etymologically analysed, *Brahman* means the all-enveloping and all-pervading principle. The term is derived from the root *vṛh* which means 'to grow, to expand, to become great'. In extended sense, therefore it means 'all-pervading'. In case of Bhartṛhari *śabda* is identified with *Brahman* because he conceives the word-principle as the basic principle of consciousness as well as the awareness of the existence of objects which are characterised by 'names' and 'forms'.

Bhartṛhari further conceives this Reality to be "without beginning and end" (*anādi nidhānam*). According to G.N. Sastri the phrase means a concept to which the qualities and attributes of 'time' cannot be applied.[3] His interpretation is justified on the following ground. All our cognitive episodes about our inner states of mind as well as the external world are sequential in nature (*krama*). They are conditioned by temporal arrangement. The word-principle being the ground of all forms of cognitions cannot be understood in terms of time, i.e., in terms of beginning and end. Hence it is without temporal sequence (*akrama*) and 'without beginning and end'. However, B.K. Matilal draws our attention to another dimension of its meaning. Following Bhartṛhari's arguments about the nature of *śabda* he very rightly points out:

> An absolute beginning of language is untenable. Language is continuous and co-terminus with human or any sentient being.[4]

According to Bhartṛhari speech is not a matter of convention made at a particular moment of time. The potency of the words to express meaning is inherent. There is some kind of natural fitness (*yogyatā*) in words to express meaning as it is the case with different sense-organs which are fit for different sense perceptions.[5] This position of Bhartṛhari is radically different from the *Nyāya* position. According to the *Nyāya* philosophers language is a matter of convention, either made by man or by God. Against this, Bhartṛhari as well as other Grammarians contend that convention itself presupposes the use of language. Bringing in God as the creator of convention is not of much help. Even God has to use some linguistic forms to formulate the convention. Therefore, the inherent potentiality of **Word** to express meaning cannot be placed in time. In this sense *śabda tattva* is eternal. The particular languages and its usages may be determined by convention, but not the concept of 'language' as such. So the use of the terms 'eternal' and 'without beginning and end' in case of Word-Principle do not lead to the assertion of a mystical entity.

However, regarding the use of the term *akṣara*, there may be some misgivings. *Akṣara* ordinarily means 'eternal'. When we define some principle as eternal it may give rise to the speculation that we are talking of some entity whose nature is in direct contrast to the momentariness of the worldly objects. According to G.N. Sastri[6] *akṣara* means 'all-pervading' as its root '**as**' implies eternity. But K.A.S. Iyer and Sukla[7] prefer to translate the term *akṣara* as phonemes. Iyer very categorically states that though the term *akṣara*, in ordinary sense, means eternal, Bhartṛhari uses the term in technical sense to mean phonemes. According to him Bhartṛhari defines *śabda tattva* as the cause of manifested phonemes. If the term *akṣara* is interpreted as 'phonemes' then it can provide certain effective clues to the understanding of the second half of the verse, — "that which appears as objects, and from whom the creation of the world proceeds". The second half of the verse seems more uncritical and mystical. For how can the **word** appear as objects ? But if *śabda* is understood as the cause of phonemes then we may drive ourselves towards a more plausible explanation.

It can very broadly be said that the **word-principle** as the embodiment of linguistic potency manifests itself as phonemes (and ultimately as language-in-use). The language in manifested form is our only way of expressing awareness about the objects as well as the activities of the world. If we withdraw this linguistic potency then there will be neither consciousness, nor cognition, nor sensation of objects. Without the application of concepts and names, objects and facts are devoid of any identity. However, to understand the true implication of the second half of the verse we need to discuss the justifications Bhartṛhari offers in support of his statement that 'the word appears as objects'. The justifications are not presented very systematically by Bhartṛhari. Sometimes they are scattered. But that should not deter us from making a critical assessment of them.

First, in his explanatory note following the opening verse, Bhartṛhari defines the objects as *śabdopagrāhī*. It implies that objects of our thought are word-determined. Be it perception, inference or any other method, whenever we cognise objects or external reality, we always do so in terms of 'names'. Without names' they are unidentifiable, hence not knowable. And our cognition, according to him are *śabdopagrāhya*, i.e., word-impregnated or intertwined with words. Both the objects and cognition being word-generated, they are conceptually dependent on **word-principle**. Objects cannot be understood without language, which in turn, is the explicit manifestation of the word-principle. Secondly, Bhartṛhari employs the logic of causality, prevalent in ancient Indian tradition, to prove that *śabda tattva* is the root of worldly manifestations. Bhartṛhari (under the verse 1.120) says:

> Just as other thinkers, while explaining causality, saw that properties of cause continue in the effects; and have declared [it] as the source of everything, either the mass of atom. . . .or primordial Matter [*pradhāna/ prakṛti*], or the collection of powers rooted in Nescience or something which has no birth nor change (but merely substratum) of appearance, in the same way in the scriptures also, the word in which the power of Enjoyer and Enjoyed are submerged has been declared to be the cause of the world in many ways.

What Bhartṛhari intends to say in the above passage can be stated in simpler terms in the following way. The attributes and qualities of cause or manifestor persist through its effects or manifestations. On the basis of observation of the nature of effects we can infer the nature of cause. For example, the curd as the effect of milk retains some of the qualities of milk. On the basis of these qualities one can infer that milk is the cause of curd, not water. Similarly on the basis of the observation of 'word-loaded' nature of phenomenal concepts we can infer that the cause of the world is of the nature of the **word**. Here, by 'others' Bhartṛhari refers to the views of *Vaiśeṣika*, *Sāṁkhya* and *Upaniṣadic* philosophy. On the basis of such a logic of causality Bhartṛhari declares:

> It is the word which sees the object, it is the word which speaks, it is the word which reveals the object which was **lying hidden** and it is on the word that the multiple word rests.[8]

In the above passage, the objects are said to be **lying hidden**. The purpose of such a description can be interpreted in the following way: the objects may exist, but their nature is not known unless and until they are subsumed under some name. This is evident from the following statement, where Bhartṛhari is more explicit:

> Even that exists is as good as non-existent as long as it does not come within the range of verbal usage. Even totally non-existent things like hare's horn or something which appears and disappears in the sky like celestial

> town (*gandharva nagara*), when brought into mind by words, figures, like something endowed with primary Reality, in various usages.[9]

This passage offers us sufficient hints about Bhartṛhari's way of looking at the word-world relationship. The function of the word is to 'mean'. But to 'mean' is not to refer to existent objects. It is not a relation if 'Fido' — Fido mould, i.e., here is the word "Fido" and there is the dog Fido. According to Bhartṛhari the words do not directly refer to the objects but to the idea or concept of the object. He is not a Realist in this sense. He rather holds that our activities in relation to the external world may be prompted by language but language does not signify them. Whatever reference is made of objects, it is always done through the 'cloak' of words.

Regarding this peculiar stand about the word-object relationship he offers further justifications. He argues that 'objects' become distinct and identifiable entities once they are subsumed under a word or name. Otherwise the world of objects is indistinguishable and an unidentifiable 'something'. In other words, distinction is made between one object and another on the basis of 'words' or names assigned to them. This position of Bhartṛhari is in direct contrast to the *Nyāya* theory of perception of objects. Gotama in *Nyāya Sūtra*, 1.1.4., considers non-verbalisability (*avyapadeśya*) as one of the characteristics of perceptual knowledge. Elaborating on this point Vātsyāyana adds, our perception need not be always associated with verbalisability. There can be non-linguistic cognition. In support of his contention he offers the example of a mute's or a child's perception. In such cases there is scope for cognition and perception but not verbalisation. So verbalisation is not an invariable condition of our knowledge of the external world. To such an objection Bhartṛhari's answer would be that 'verbalisation' and 'verbalisability' are not identical-concepts. Our perceptual cognition need not always be presented in articulate verbal form. But that does not preclude the possibility of the potency for linguistic expressibility. Even the bare awareness of object is not possible without its being potent with cognitive discriminations (*pratyavamarśa*). When we fail to subsume our awareness of objects under a name, we understand them with the help of words 'this' or 'that'. Therefore, without cognitive discrimination there is no object. The discrimination is possible through conceptualisation, and conceptualisation is penetrated (*anuviddha*) by words.[10]

All these justifications presented in preceding pages are used by Bhartṛhari to vindicate his metaphysical position that "the words create the objects". His arguments shows no trace of obscurity. It is metaphysically cogent and coherent. He takes the concept of *Śabda tattva* as basic and primary. It rather works like a pair of tinged spectacles. Whichever way he looks it appears to be tinged with linguistic potency. But this cannot be considered to be a defect in metaphysics, rather this is the way of doing metaphysics. The metaphysician has only one tool in his hand, i.e., the **concept**. He puts emphasis on this or that concept as the primary one and accordingly his conceptual scheme takes shape. In case of Bhartṛhari *śabda* is the primary concept. With the help of this he develops a non-dualistic (*advaita*) and holistic world-view.

Problems of Linguistic Monism

We must now examine how successfully Bhartṛhari handles the problem of bridging the gap between plurality and unity. This is the greatest challenge for any Monistic philosopher. Bhartṛhari's task seem to be more difficult, for his metaphysical Reality is of the nature of **Word**. So he has the double task of bridging the gap between the **Word** and existence, and between the one and the many.

He explains the empirical level of existence with the help of certain key concepts. They are: (1) Consciousness/awareness, (2) concepts, (3) existence of objects, and (4) change. So our first job will be to examine these four concepts from Bhartṛhari's standpoint. In the process, we are likely to notice a peculiar feature of Bhartṛhari's method. At each level of his conceptual exploration he exhibits that differentiation implies unity.

(a) Word and Consciousness

Let us start by examining what Bhartrhari means by consciousness or awareness. We, as conscious beings are aware of the innumerable factual events and objects around us. We are aware of them not because of sense perception, but because we can cognise them as distinct and particular things subsumable under different names and forms. So according to him there can be no cognitive awareness without its being intertwined with words. If we take away this property of "word-loadedness" from cognition then no cognitive awareness is worth its name. In other words, **word** and consciousness are inseparably related. Of course from such an account it should not be presumed that Bhartṛhari means by consciousness a form of "inner speech". Being conscious does not mean we are constantly in the process of using words. Nor does he attach primacy to language over thought. Bhartṛhari, himself, is aware of the two different ways of interpreting the relationship between the words and consciousness. He states that according to some, there cannot be consciousness without words. Consciousness and words are two distinct phenomena, but words have primacy over consciousness because consciousness is not possible without words. Others, on the other hand, hold that consciousness is just this fact of being the word-potent. The two are identical. Though Bhartṛhari does not clearly mention his preference in the verse, yet from the verse 1.118 it is clear that he accepts the latter view. He says: "what is called awareness (consciousness), i.e., *samjñā*, is having the form of speech or words (*vāgrupatā*). Consciousness in all beings never goes beyond it, that is, it is never different from the fact of having the form of the word". We only become aware of the difference between them when the words are expressed in sequential and articulate manner to express our thought. It should be noted in this connection that he makes a clear distinction between the particular linguistic episodes, i.e., when words and phonemes are in particular sequential order; and the inherent linguistic potency in all consicous beings, which has the latent power to be expressed as particular linguistic statements.

(b) Word and Concept

The next problem that needs attention is Bhartṛhari's view of concepts'. It is usually believed that all words do not represent concepts. Only class names like 'cow', 'horse', 'beautiful', 'red', etc. are conceptualisable and hence they stand for universals. Concepts are formed on the basis of some common attributes shared by the members of the class. But Bhartṛhari's notion of 'concept' is quite different. He believes that all words are universal, so all the words stand for concepts. Following Matilal's interpretation we can say that for Bhartṛhari "words and concepts are merely two sides of a same coin".[11] Therefore in Bhartṛhari's epistemological scheme there cannot be any non-conceptual (*nirvikalpaka*) awareness. For all forms of awareness imply the presence of words. And all words, in turn, are concepts. Even the terms like 'this' or 'that' which are ordinarily believed to signify pure particulars (something which cannot be brought under the range of description), are also regarded as universal by Bhartṛhari. The reason for such a non-conventional view is due to his analysis of meaning in term of 'sense' rather than 'reference'. Therefore, he considers 'sentences' as the primary units of meaning, not the words. In case of linguistic communication it is the 'sense' which is expressed by speaker and grasped by the hearer. So he does not face any problem in explaining all forms of words in terms of concepts and universals. He does not analyse sentences in terms of '**that**' and '**what**'. In such a scheme of analysis, the '**that**' of the subject refers to the pure particular which is qualified by the '**what**' of the quality or universal attributes. For Bhartṛhari words can only refer to the universal of objects.

(c) Word Universal and Object Universal

Still one knotty problem remains. Bhartṛhari talks of two kinds of universals, i.e., the universal of words and the universal objects. How are these two universals connected by Bhartṛhari ? To understand this problem we will have to clarify the sense in which he uses the terms 'words' and 'objects'/ 'referents'. In his analysis of 'language-in-use' he makes a distinction between the expressed (*vācya*) and the expressive word (*vācaka*). The *vācaka* expresses the meaning and meaning implies the object meant. But objects meant, are never directly grasped by the words. The particulars of the world are never knowable. The words always mean the universal of the objects. Whatever we know of the objects is known through the universalised concepts (*vikalpas*). For Bhartṛhari these universals do not exist in the objects. Whatever we know of the objects is through the 'cloak' of words. The universal of the words and the universal of things, both are word-generated, hence there is no opposition between them. He transforms the 'word-universals' to 'thing-universals' to explain the existence of the world.

The Notion of Change and Time

So from our discussion we find that for Bhartṛhari : (1) consciousness and word are identical, (2) concepts and words are identical, (3) the universal of the objects and the universal of words are identical. In fact, all the diversities of concepts that we have discussed are significant in the empirical level of 'use'. But at the conceptual level they are non-different, one and the ultimate idea, i.e., the word-principle. The diversity of phenomenal level is accommodated within the principle of the one *śabda tattva* without any trace of quality or opposition. Now let us take up for examination another important concept, i.e., change. We shall have to deal with this concept at two levels : (i) How does the one Reality transforms itself into the phenomenal level of plurality ? In other words, the change from the transcendental to phenomenal; (ii) The nature of change that characterises the world of particularities.

The first issue regarding the transformation of the transcendental to phenomenal is sought to be solved by the theory of causation. Bhartṛhari himself says in the 1st verse of *Vākyapadīya* that, "from the *śabda Brahman* the creation proceeds". In the Indian philosophical tradition those who subscribe to the view that "effect is cause transformed", are called *satkāryavādins*. Hence Bhartṛhari's view comes under the fold of the above theory. But, again the theory has been interpreted in two ways. Those who believe that the effect is the real transformation of the cause, are called *pariṇāmavādins*. According to them the cause changes its nature to become the effect, whereas the *vivartavādins* are of opinion that the transformation from the cause to the effect is apparent. The nature of the cause remains unchanged, and cause is non-different from the effect. The *Advaitins*, especially Śaṅkara, is the chief protagonist of the latter theory. There is no unanimity of opinion amongst modern scholars as to the real nature of Bhartṛhari's theory of causation. Bhartṛhari's use of the term *vivartate* in the introductory verse seems to settle the issue. But the issue cannot be settled on the basis of the use of this term. G.N. Sastri raises a valid objection. He very rightly points out: "It appears to us. . . that Bhartṛhari was not familiar with the difference in connotations of two terms (*pariṇāma* and *vivarta*) which is usual in later philosophical literature".[12] He and Ms. Biardeau[13] feel that Bhartṛhari has not interpreted the transformation of the world from the word in the light of *vivartavāda*, (as the term is understood by the *Advaitins*). They argue that such interpretations found in the *vṛttis* were incorporated by later Grammarians. The basis of their argument is that *Vṛttis* of *Vākyapadīya* was not done by Bhartṛhari but by Harivṛṣabha and Puṇyarāja. These later Grammarians belonged to post-Śaṅkarite period. But K.A.S. Iyer[14] and B.K.Matilal[15] are of opinion that

Bhartṛhari offers a *vivartavādin* interpretation of the nature of transformation.

It seems that the controversy cannot be resolved so easily, for there is no conclusive proof available regarding real authorship of the *Vṛttis*. So let us look at the problem from another angle. Let us go back to what Bhartṛhari says about his philosophical approach. He claims that as a Grammarian he is not interested in what the facts present, but what the language presents. In his metaphysical scheme he seems to translate this basic line of approach at every stage. He looks at every problem and concept through the key-hole of language. So he is not bothered about the physical element of existence and creation. All the ideas associated with the empirical world, such as 'objects', 'substancehood', 'particularity' are interpreted by him in terms of **Word**. This provides a strong evidence for the view that Bhartṛhari subscribed to *vivartavāda*. The world is the apparent manifestation of the Word-Principle. The *śabda Brahman* does not transform itself to become the world.

Coming to another meaning of change, i.e., the change at the empirical level, we find that Bhartṛhari introduces the concept of time (*kāla*) to explain the problem. In *Vākyapadīya,* I.2, he says: "*śabda Brahman* though one has many powers and one of them is the power of time (*kālaśakti*)." These powers are actually non-different from the *śabda Brahman*. It is due to our ignorance, we conceive these powers as different from the ultimate Reality. It is obvious that he introduces the concept of diverse powers of the Reality to explain the diverse ways in which we use language to describe the world. Instead of treating these various categories of linguistic presentation as representing the categories of existing things (*dravya*), as is done by the *Vaiśeṣikas*, he prefers to call them the attributes of Reality. *Śabda Brahman* as the causal ground of the phenomenal world must include within its conceptual range the various categories used for thinking and talking about the empirical world.

The concept of Time has been discussed in detail in the III *Kāṇḍa* of Bhartṛhari's *Vākyapadīya,* wherein he devotes an entire section to Time (*Kāla samuddeśa*). His views on 'Time' can be summed up as follows:

> The reality called *Brahman*, is without any sequence and consists of True knowledge and it is not affected by Time. Under the influence of Nescience, it assumes sequence and appears as this or that. Thus, through the interventions of Time the phenomena appear in a temporal sequence to the individual selves coming down from time immemorial. Because all differentiation consists of Nescience, all division of Time, adopted from different points of view, are also the creations of Nescience. Once True knowledge dawns, all differentiation disappears and, therefore, this division (of Time) also disappears. Therefore to discuss whether it (division) is right or not, would result in labour only.[16]

Thus Helārāja sums up Bhartṛhari's views on Time. Bhartṛhari also conceives Time as the efficient cause (*nimitta kāraṇa*) and it is attributed with the power of production (*abhyanujña*) and obstruction (*pratibandha*) of particular things of the world.

It sometimes appears that Bhartṛhari indulges in a metaphysics of time rather than offering us an analysis of the concept of 'Time' with relation to the word-world relationship. It also sometimes seems to express his mystical leanings. Therefore it directly goes against his avowed claim that his philosophical analysis is based on "what language presents". But if we overlook some of these mystical descriptions we may find a logic behind Bhartṛhari's emphasis on the concept of Time. He introduces this concept to explain another important dimension of the phenomenal world, i.e., the idea of 'change'. Explaining the idea of multiplicity is not enough for providing a correct analysis of the empirical phenomena. He conceives of the Reality as **one** and **unchangeable**. The phenomenal world being characterised by change owes an explanation in terms of the unchangeable Reality. To explain this issue Bhartṛhari introduces Time. In certain respects Bhartṛhari's description of *kālaśakti* is similar to that of Saṅkara's conception of *māyā*. Both the concepts signify the power of introducing multiplicity and change at the phenomenal level. Yet there is a difference between the conception of *kāla* and *māyā*. *Māyā* is seen from two angles; in its projective form it is *māyā,* and in its negative form it is *avidyā*. But for Bhartṛhari *kāla* is conceived because of *avidyā*. *Kāla* itself is not *avidyā*. Moreover *kāla* is directly related to his explanation of every diversity at the linguistic level. Our experience, cognitions as well as the awareness of objects are intertwined with words. They are conceivable and communicable in terms of language. And all forms of linguistic expressibility imply the presentation of the phonemes and syllables in sequential pattern. In case of our linguistic utterances we utter them syllable by syllable. We cannot express the whole meaning at one point of time. So sequence (*krama*) is an important aspect of speech. Similarly, our experiences — be it of external world or inner states of our mind, such as pleasure, pain etc. — are arranged in time. Otherwise we cannot distinguish one experience from the other. As Bhartṛhari analyses the phenomenal world in terms of *śabda*, for him the sequential presentation of words is very important. So he conceives Time as the **a-priori** condition of our thought, knowledge and speech. This aspect of Time proves the difference between Śaṅkara's view of *māyā* and Bhartṛhari's view of *kāla*. Śaṅkara has no compulsion for explaining the phenomena in terms of sequence.

Another important aspect of his emphasis on Time is brought to light by Helārāja in his *Vṛtti*.[17] This, to a large extent supports Bhartṛhari's approach to philosophy in terms of *śabdenābhidhiyate*. He says that the main purpose of Bhartṛhari in devoting a whole section of his book to Time is not to define it philosophically but to analyse some problems with regard to the use of verbs in different tenses. One problem already discussed in the *Mahābhāṣya* is — how can the present tense be used in regard to eternal things ? Another question that crops up is with regard to the use of two words expressive of two different tenses in the same sentence. Innumerable problems may arise in connection with the use of tense forms. These tense forms cannot be understood without reference to Time. Besides all our linguistic expressions refer either to the past or to the present or to the future. They represent the arrangement of events in Time. Therefore Bhartṛhari conceives Time as the effective cause of the phenomenal world.

Helārāja's exposition of this of particular dimension of Bhartṛhari's conception of Time, atleast, removes our misgivings about the inconsistency committed by him. It confirms that Bhartṛhari's approach to philosophy is Word-oriented, not Existence-oriented. He is concerned with the explanation of the nature of Time as far as it comes within the purview of the linguistic representation of the Realtity.

Now we are in a better position to understand the basic tenets of Bhartṛhari's Monism. The *śabda Brahman* as the Reality is presented here as the ultimate ground of unity. This unity is not forced upon the level of diversity, for the diversities at each level point to unity.

(1) At the level of language-in-use, there is a presupposed unity amongst the form of words, meaning and the referent. As long as language is not manifested and expressed, we cannot differentiate these three elements. They are present within us in the form of an undifferentiated **one**.

(2) At the level of consciousness there is the unity between the universal of the word and the universal of things. Only when the words are used we differentiate between the universal elements in the word and the objects-meant.

(3) At the level of cognition the diverse elements of objects of reference, actions and relations are united and cognised in an unitary form. In our statements about cognition there is reference to the objects, qualities, relations etc. Conceptually they are distinguishable but in the sentence they are united.

All these levels of unity presuppose an ultimate unity by virtue of the fact that they are all word-potent. This common element of word-potency is crystallised in our conception of *śabda tattva*, the ultimate Reality. This is how Bhartṛhari presents a consistent account of the relation between the one and the many; the unity and the multiplicity.

Bhartṛhari's Monism and Its Logical Conclusions

Our discussion on Bhartṛhari's metaphysics of language will not be complete without a review of the logical conclusion that follows from his Monism. Depending upon the nature of the basic concepts each philosophical system leads to the formation of a world-view. Such world-views may be Conceptualistic, Realistic, Phenomenalistic or Nominalistic. Bhartṛhari's Linguistic Monism leads him to Phenomenalistic and Holistic world-view

Let us first of all examine — what sort of logical picture we can form about the world if it is seen from the platform of 'language' ? To get an answer to the question, we have to know how Bhartṛhari presents the concept of language-in-use. According to him language-in-use is a vehicle of communicating the meaning. But the meanings that are expressed by particular sentences or the words cannot be considered to present the **Meaning** as a whole. The diverse ways we express meaning can at best give us a 'piece' or a 'bit' of the **Meaning-whole**. When we use language for communication we extract a 'part' of it on the basis of selecting what we intend to express. This is done by the method of, what Bhartṛhari calls, *apoddhāra*, i.e., "the process of constant and progressive extraction, comparison, analysis and abstraction".[18] The meaning is attached to these abstracted 'bits', extracted from the linguistic-whole by abstracting letters from the words, words from the sentences, sentences from the discourse, and discourses from the larger discourse and so on. These 'bits' of meaning presented by words, sentences and discourses owe their significance to the **Meaning-whole** or the **Real-word**, which Bhartṛhari designates as the *sphoṭa*. The *sphoṭa* is the operative ground of our linguistic communication. This is the unified point which includes the word, the form of the word and the meaning. At the level of *sphoṭa*, all these elements are undifferentiated. Each conscious being share this unitary *sphoṭa*. Therefore, the speaker can express his thought in unlimited number of ways and mean innumerable objects. Similarly, the hearer can understand the speaker because he shares the same store-house of meaning. So each linguistic expression is nothing but only a part of the expressible **Meaning-essence** or **Meaning-whole**.

When we employ the extracted 'bits' of meaning, we also refer to the extracted 'bits' of the phenomenal world. Corresponding to the 'whole' of meaning, there is a 'whole' of the objects-meant. The world of objects as such is not knowable. We only know a 'bit' of it as is presented by sentences and words. Whatever we know of the objects is limited by concepts — the linguistic constructs (*vikalpa*). The concepts involve the process of selection and elimination. For example, the word *ghaṭa* (pot) as a concept can only mean a part of the object referred to, namely the universal of *ghaṭatva* (potness). But the particular object referred to, can be described and meant in innumerable ways. We can as well refer to the pot's redness by the sentence 'the pot is red'. If one wants to refer to the colour of the pot then he has to use the concept 'redness'. So the 'whole' of the object cannot be grasped by the language. The object can be 'meant' differently with reference to different words that express it. In each case we present a selected and limited aspect of it. The 'whole of objects-meant' and the 'whole of the meaning' are ungraspable by the 'bits' of the linguistic units.

Logical Atomism and Holism

In this connection, it will be of interest to examine the Logical Atomism of Russell and Wittgenstein. Of course, the *Vaiśeṣika* system of India presents an Atomistic world-view. But their metaphysical position is quite different. They are Realists, and they do not look at facts from the stand point of language. Coming back to Logical Atomism, we note that Wittgenstein (of *Tractatus*) conceives that the language and the reality (world) share the same logical structure. So by ayalysing the logical structure of language, we can unravel the logical structure of reality. According to Russell and early Wittgenstein, to determine the logic of the language we must analyse it into its simplest and unanalysable form. The simplest form of linguistic statement is the atomic proposition. These atomic propositions picture the simplest and unanalysable facts, called 'the atomic facts'. These atomic propositions, according to them, are not further analysable into proposition but to the elements, called the 'logical proper names'. And these logical proper names refer to the simplest element of reality called 'objects'. So at the linguistic level, the ultimate unit is the 'proper name' which corresponds to the ultimate unit of referents, i.e., 'objects'. These 'objects' are neither objectively nor ontologically determined. They are logical and are assumed in the context of the logical analysis of language. With this interpretation of the relation between word and world, Wittgenstein and Russell successfully overcame the problem of relating physical things to the words. Here, the nature of the reality is determined in terms of the logical analysis of language. We find that both Bhartṛhari and the Logical Atomists analyse the structure of the world in terms of the structure of language. Both analyse language through the method of abstraction. But for Bhartṛhari the whole is real whereas the abstracted and analysed 'bits' are unreal and artificial. But for the Logical Atomists the abstracted unit is logically real but the whole cannot represent the real. For Bhartṛhari the whole is indivisible whereas for the Logical Atomists the ultimately abstracted 'bit' is indivisible and unanalysable. So their logical conclusion is entirely different from Bhartṛhari's. The entire analysis of the Logical Atomists leads to a form of Referential theory of meaning. For the logical proper names must be hooked to the referent — 'object'. The atomic propositions are a picture of atomic facts. In a sense, logically there are two parallel levels — the level of facts and the level of language, bound by the common logical structure. But in Bhartṛhari's theory the level of referents and the level of language are non-differentiable, as the referents and facts are not analysable except through language.

In Bhartṛhari's metaphysical scheme there is no scope for duality. So the world of objects and the world of words cannot be cognised independent of one another. But Bhartṛhari, at the same time does not deny the existence of empirical world independent of cognition. What he simply means is that the true nature of the existence is beyond the scope of cognition. Cognition being word-potent can frame the picture of the objects as it is presented through words. The objects are known only through the 'guise' of words. The real existence (*mukhya sattā*) is unknowable. But it exists, for all our activities prompted by language deal with external realities. Otherwise our activities would not be possible. "Being asked for food we cannot very well present the speaker's 'mental' food".[19] Then why does Bhartṛhari believe that we can only know the objects as represented by words ? In answer Bhartṛhari would say "It is extremely difficult to establish by reasoning the nature of objects, because the properties differ according to difference in circumstances, place and time" (I.32.). So the objecs are understood so far as they are caught within the network of the universal of words. And we transfer the universal of the words to thing-universals. So objects have a metaphorical existence (*upacāra sattā*). The attributes of words are metaphorically superimposed on objects.

Quine would call such an explication of the relation between the word and the object as a non-critical and primitive way of looking at things. He says: "you and I never confuse physical things with their names, but primitive people do view names as somehow the soul or the essence of the thing".[20] But in case of Bhartṛhari such criticism would not apply, for Bhartṛhari is not confusing names with the essences of things. For him whatever we can know of the objects is how it is presented to us by the words. His position is in this sense is Nominalistic, i.e., we know the things as they are represented by the names and words. B.K. Matilal very aptly points out that in the philosophy of Bhartṛhari there is no confusion, but 'fusion'[21] between the words or names and the object. So words and the meanings are regarded as non-distinct prior to their manifestation. The manifested form of articulate words illuminate the meanings for the hearer to grasp, and then it becomes superimposed and identified with the things. According to Bhartṛhari's viewpoint there is no fallacy involved in saying 'This is a cow' instead of saying "This is the object which we call a member of the cow-class". "This **fusion** of sign and object constitutes an important part of what language actually is".[22] Bhartṛhari would call this **'attributive** identification' or 'identification through attribution' or 'superimposition' (*adhyavasāya*).[23]

Thus Bhartṛhari offers us a Metaphysics of Word — which is conceived by him to be the principle of ultimate unity. It is such a form of unity which allows the possibility of differentiation and division. But these divisions and differentiations are not logically independent, as they imply unity as their explanatory principle. They have significance only with reference to the empirical and phenomenal. But for those who have achieved the knowledge, the essence of language, the phenomenal divisions of concepts and forms have no real significance. Therefore, according to Bhartṛhari the study of *Vyākaraṇa* is the doorway to liberation.

References

1. K.A.S. Iyer, *Vākyapadīya,* Pt. I.
2. B.K. Matilal, *The Word and the World,* p. 85.
3. Gourinath Sastri, *A Study in The Dialectics of Sphoṭa,* Delhi: Motilal Banarsidass, 1980, p.x.
4. Matilal, *The Word and the World,* p. 125.
5. *Vākyapadīya,* I.97.
6. Gourinath Sastri, *Dialectics of Sphoṭa,* p.x.
7. S.N. Sukla, *Vākyapadīya Bhāvapradīpa,* Chowkhamba, 1961.
8. *Vākyapadīya, Vṛtti* under I.118, tr. by Iyer, p. 106.
9. *Ibid., Vṛtti* under I.121, tr. by Iyer, p. 109.

10. *Vākyapadīya*, I.124-25.
11. Matilal, *Perception*, Oxford: Clarendon Press, 1986, p. 393.
12. G.N. Sastri, *The Philosophy of Word and Meaning*, Calcutta : Sanskrit College, 1969, p. 56.
13. M. Biardeau, *Vākyapadīya*, *Brahmakāṇḍa*, French translation, Introduction.
14. Iyer, *Bhartṛhari*, p. 130.
15. Matilal, *Perception*, p. 195.
16. As translated by Iyer, *Bhartṛhari*, p. 123.
17. *Vāk*, pt. III. Pt. II. I.25-27.

    nāsmābhidarśanavivekaḥ prārabdhvaḥ I *kintu śabda vyavahāra yadangaṃ tatparikṣyaṃ* I *asti ca bhinnakālaḥ śābdo vyavahāro'bhudasti bhaviṣyatitī* I *tatra yathāyogamvicāritaramaṇiyaḥ kālo' bhyupantavya idarthaḥ.*

18. Matilal, *Perception*, p. 393.
19. Matilal, *Word and World*, p. 129.
20. W.V.O. Quine, "Mind and Verbal dispositions", In *Mind and Language*, ed. by S. Gutten Plan, p. 50 quotation taken from Matilal's *Perception*, p. 396.
21. Matilal, *Perception*, p. 397.
22. *Ibid.*
23. *Ibid.*

    Helāraja's commentary on *Jāti Samuddeśa*, 6. Quoted from Matilal, *Perception*, p. 397.

3

The *Sphoṭa* Theory of Language

Language Analysis and Metaphysics

THE concept of *sphoṭa* as the ultimate principle of linguistic communication is unique and novel in many respects. Matilal very rightly points out that "the Indian grammarians' theory of *sphoṭa* has been acclaimed as one of the most important contributions to central problem of general linguistics as well as philosophy of language".[1] However, the worth of such a theory has for a long time remained unnoticed. It is only with the revival of interest in philosophy of language, that the *sphoṭa* theory has come to the limelight. The concept of *sphoṭa* is not originally offered by Bhartṛhari. But it cannot be denied that it was he who used it as the fundamental concept of the study of language. Later Grammarians have successfully developed the theory further. But have done so only on the basis of the ground work provided by Bhartṛhari.

It is unfortunate that some early Indologists like Keith[2] and De[3] have described the concept of *sphoṭa* as a mystical entity. A careful study of Bhartṛhari's analysis does not show much trace of mysticism. Some analogies and epithets used by Bhartṛhari may create such impression. But such instances are rare. Rather his analysis and explanation through metaphors are clear and straightforward. Under no circumstances can we interpret them as mystical. According to some modern thinkers such wrong ascription of mysticism may be due to his theory of *śabda tattva Brahman*. If such is the case, then it shows the strong bias of the critics and interpreters against Bhartṛhari. It may be also due to the misconception that any talk about the **Reality** in metaphysical sense is another way of indulging in mysticism. If so, then all the theories of the past in India, as well as in the West, can be bundled off as mysticism. Even the concept of 'Absolute' of Hegel and Bradley, the Logical Atomism of Russell, will not be spared from the charge of mysticism. But this is not the case, as is evident from large volumes of critical writings available on all these philosophers and metaphysicians.

Coming back to Bhartṛhari's theory of *sphoṭa*, we may note that this is more a part of his philosophy of language than the metaphysics of language. In spite of some metaphysical underpinnings his philosophy of language is theoretically autonomous. Rather, after going through his philosophical analysis of language-in-use, one may be left with the impression that his concept of *śabda Brahman* draws its logical support from the former and not the *vice-versa*. And the theory of *sphoṭa* is the anchor sheet of his inquiry about 'how language functions' ? This inquiry utlimately leads him to the conception of Reality in the form of *śabda tattva*. Passing from language analysis to metaphysics is not a new thing. There are plenty of instances in the history of philosophy where the notion of language implicitly or explicitly has determined the nature of metaphysical theories. The phenomenon of language has always perplexed the critical thinkers of the past. The questions like — what after all is language ? How do we express our thoughts through language ? Whether language can offer us some clue to the understanding of human experience and cognition etc., contine to haunt the philosophers. Therefore, we come across many metaphysical theories which are largely determined by one's speculations about the nature of language. Plato, for example, finds a clue to the solution of the riddle of Being and Becoming by looking at the nature of the words that are used in our cognitive episodes. He finds that the words that signify concepts remain unchanged amidst the fluctuations in the level of experienceable facts of the world. Unless the concepts and names are taken to be objective, universal and stable, no thought, no judgements about the nature of the world would be possible. The words and concepts go on conveying the same meaning in spite of the variations and changes in the level of the referred objects. Therefore he offers the status of **Reality** to universal class names. He calls them 'Ideas'. Aristotle on the other hand, looks at the nature of judgements and their linguistic expressions to pinpoint the basic categories through which our mind understands the facts. Out of ten such categories he offers primacy to substance and quality. These two categories are represented by the subject and predicate of judgements. These two primary linguistic elements are turned into the metaphysical principles of 'form' and 'matter'. Russell very rightly observes that Artistotle transforms the simple linguistic fact of subject and predicate into metaphysical Realities. Kant, another gifted and original philosopher of the West, escapes the metaphysical trap of the Platonic and Aristotelian kind. But in his *Critique of Pure Reason,* he analyses the judgemental forms to delienate the structural map of the 'knowable'. His categories of understanding, which according to him are the *a-priori* conditions of the knowable and experienceable, are in fact drawn from the forms of judgement. But he avoids turning them into transcendental Realities. His metaphysics is different. It is not transcendental metaphysics but, as he claims, the 'metaphysics of experience'. Strawson analysing it further shows that Kant's is a form of 'Descriptive Metaphysics'—which instead of offering a revised conceptual order, draws its principal materials from the actual way of describing the world.

So, we notice that the analysis of linguistic forms and principles have many a times determined the metaphysical stand of a philosopher. Bhartṛhari's way of doing metaphysics is not an exception to the rule. What makes Bhartṛhari a philosopher of different kind is his deliberate and explicit effort to explicate every concept in terms of linguistic facts. No doubt, he begins his treatiste with the announcement about the ultimate metaphysical Reality, but it is entirely based on the workings of language at the phenomenal level. Like the twentieth century philosophers of language, his chief concern is to examine 'how language functions' at different levels of our conscious activity. 'Language' is the only 'object' as well as the only 'means' of doing philosophy. So we need not always drag in the metaphysical concept of *śabda tattva* to understand what he has to say about the nature of language and linguistic communication.

At the outset I must mention that the concept of *sphoṭa* is very much a part of his philosophy of language. Though sometimes he uses the terms *śabda* and *sphoṭa* interchangeably, the contexts of his statements make it clear that in such cases *śabda* does not mean *śabda-Brahman.* The concept of *sphoṭa* is presented by him as the ultimate ground of the linguistic communicability. It is the co-ordinating factor amongst the varying aspects of language-in-use.

Sphoṭa : Its Meaning aad Implications

It is very difficult to translate the term *sphoṭa* into English. It has been varyingly translated as the 'Real-word', 'Logos', 'Real Language', the 'Bearer of meaning' etc. Things will be easier if we explain it etymologically. The term *sphoṭa* is taken from the root *sphuṭ* which means 'bursting forth' or which has a tendency to manifest itself. Nāgeśa Bhaṭṭa, a follower of Bhartṛhari, describes *sphoṭa* in two ways — that from which meaning bursts forth, and thus is the meaning-bearer; and the principle which is manifested through phonemes. By no means, Bhartṛhari is the first philosopher to use the term *sphoṭa*. Its etymological history dates back to Pāṇini's reference to the term *sphoṭayana* in his treatise *Aṣṭādhyāyī*.[4] Haradatta,[5] the follower of Pāṇini believed that Sphoṭāyana was the first propounder of the *sphoṭa* doctrine. Yāska,[6] however refers to another ancient scholar Adumbarāyaṇa, who propounded the philosophy of *sphoṭa*. John Brough[7] is of opinion that in all probability Adumbarāyaṇa was the forerunner of Bhartṛhari's theory of *sphoṭa*. However, it was Patañjali who explicitly discusses about *sphoṭa* in his *Mahābhāṣya*.[8] According to him *sphoṭa* signifies speech/language, and the audible sound (*dhvani*) is its special quality. The audible noise may be variable depending on the speaker's mode of utterance, whereas *sphoṭa* as the unit of speech is not subject to such variations. But Bhartṛhari develops the idea of *sphoṭa* in a completely different way. He ascribes to it an unique philosophical dimension. For him *sphoṭa* is neither a meaning-bearing unit nor a linguistic sign. It is something more than that. The true implication of Bhartṛhari's version of *sphoṭa* theory will be clearer as we proceed with our discussions.

The question that needs some elaboration, at this stage of our discussion is — why does Bhartṛhari talk of *sphoṭa* as the primary basis of all sorts of deliberations on the nature of language ? To answer this, we must first of all identify all the elements involved in case of our linguistic expressions. Language-in-use involves a complex network of elementary factors. First, our linguistic utterance involves the use of audible noise through vocal organ. But any and every audible noise is not language. The sounds and syllables uttered have a form of their own, which only make some audible sounds a part of language. Then comes the question of meaning that is expressed through the audible sound patterns. It also involves the ordering of sound forms and words in a particular order. In other words, without the rules of grammar and syntax meaning is not articulately expressible. Again the words and sentences that are uttered, are supposed to have an object of reference, i.e., a 'designate'. If we probe still further, we notice that linguistic utterances imply the notion of a speaker, who primarily and essentially uses language to express his thought and intention. But the process of linguistic act will be valueless if there is no hearer to understand what the speaker means to say. Atleast, all these factors mentioned above must be explained to offer a complete account of how language works. For Bhartṛhari language is not simply analysable in terms of phonetics, syntax, grammar and semantics. Language is above all, meant for communication. It is inter-subjective, where both the speaker and the hearer have an active role to play. Therefore, Bhartṛhari takes care to analyse the multiple nuances of language. Not only he explains these varied dimensions of 'language' but offers a coherent account of it. Here the concept of *sphoṭa* is needed to provide an anchor-sheet to the complex activity called language. Bhartṛhari begins his discussion on the nature of language by distinguishing two aspects of language. In verse I.44 he says in any case of meaningful linguistic utterance (expressive word) the experts on language comprehend two elements. One is the root cause of manifestation (*nimitta*), and the other is the applied (*prajujyate*), when manifested, to convey meaning. The latter element is called *sphoṭa* and the former is *nāda/ dhvani. Sphoṭa* is the real basis of language, the very linguistic potency, which is manifested by *dhvani. Dhvani* is the audible sound pattern, wihout which the very potency of meaning and its expressibility is impossible. That is why the audible speech, which is presented sequentially syllable by syllable, is called the *nimitta* (cause) of the manifested meaningful expression. The *sphoṭa* is defined as indivisible, partless, sequenceless whole. All the grammatical and syntactical divisions are discernible only when the thought is translated into the audible sound pattern. At this stage, the language becomes applicable, because along with the phonetic elements it also expresses the meaning. The unit of meaning, expressed by the sound pattern, is there in the verbal dispositional ability of the speaker as well as the hearer. In his commentary on the verse I.44 he says :

> "In the sequenceless nature of the *vāk* (speech) [which also means *sphoṭa*] both the powers, the power to be articulated in sound (audible form) and the power to convey meaning, lie intermixed.[9]

In spite of the risk of misrepresentation we can interpret the *sphoṭa* and *dhvani* distinction in terms of the distinction between the propositional content and the speech-act. I bring in the term 'propositional content' to make it clear that according to Bhartṛhari the same *sphoṭa* can be expressed in different languages, like English, Sanskrit, etc. Yet it will be wrong to say that *sphoṭa* is the 'bearer of meaning'. *Sphoṭa* implies the total 'unit of linguistic potency' — which when expressed is diversified into two elements, sound-word and meaning-word. The entire idea can be expressed clearly with the help of the following diagram.

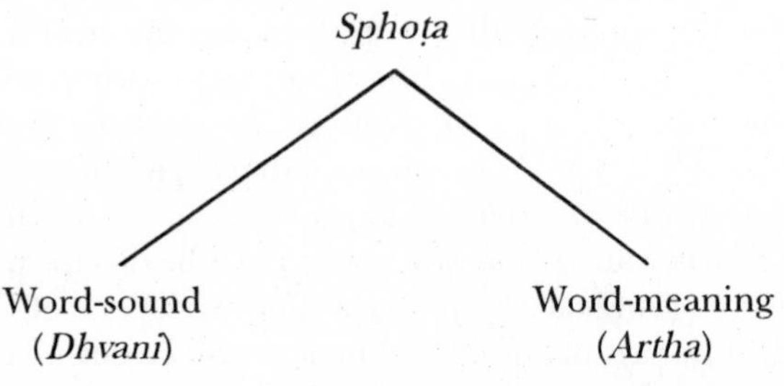

From the above diagram, it follows that the indivisible, changeless *sphoṭa* is a two-sided coin. One of its dimension is the sound pattern and the other is meaning-bearing unit. It is believed that *sphoṭa* along with expressing the meaning also expresses itself. This is expressed by Bhartṛhari in the following way, under the verse I.46:

> Just as light/fire (*jyoti*) resides in the *araṇi* (Churning) stick and (being manifested becomes the cause for manifesting other object; *śabda* resides likewise in the MIND (*Buddhi*, the inner faculty) and being manifested becomes separately the cause for manifesting itself as well as the meaning.[10]

The concept of *sphoṭa* has been explained by Bhartṛhari through many such analogies. They sometimes, lead to confusion regarding the exact significance of this term. So we come across varied interpretation of the meaning of the term. There is no unanimity of opinion regarding the exact significance of *sphoṭa* amidst the scholars. John Brough and K. Kunjunni Raja interpret *sphoṭa* as the linguistic sign in its meaning-bearing aspect. According to Joshi[11] and Caradona[12] *sphoṭa* should mean sound unit of the language system. Iyer,[13] however, refutes the latter view and argues that *sphoṭa* should include the meaning-bearing speech unit. I feel that Matilal offers the most balanced and plausible explanation of what Bhartṛhari means by *sphoṭa*. According to him "*sphoṭa* is the real substratum, proper linguistic unit, which is identical also with its meaning. Language is not the vehicle of meaning or the conveyor belt of thought. Thought anchors language and language anchors the thought. *Śabdanā*, 'languageing' is, thinking; and thought vibrates through language. In this way of looking at things, there cannot be any essential difference between a linguistic unit and its meaning or the thought it conveys. *Sphoṭa* refers to this non-differentiated language-principle.''[14]

Now let us see why the concept of *sphoṭa* as the 'language-principle' is presupposed by Bhartṛhari. He could have done away with such a concept and could have carried on his discussions about language in term of the words and the meanings. What exactly is the role of *sphoṭa* in our understanding of the nature of language ? To justify Bhartṛhari's need for introduction of the concept of *sphoṭa*, we should still go deeper into the analysis of how language functions. And on the basis of this we can offer justifications for Bhartṛhari's need for assuming the idea of *sphoṭa*.

One of the questions that baffles the philosophers of language is connected with the human ability to formulate and understand unlimited variations in linguistic expressions.

> There are limitless sentences and combinations of sentences of which we know, in advance, the sense, the significance; though we shall only over use, or hear or read, a comparatively insignificant portion of them.

So "we ask: how is it that we have vast and potentially limitless understanding'' ?[15] Strawson, one of the most eminent philosopher of our times, formulates the problem for the modern philosophy of language in the above manner. It is obvious that this vital issue of the language-speakers limitless ways of expressing thoughts must have bothered Bhartṛhari and the ancient Indian Grammarians too. Though the nature of the problem is same for both Bhartṛhari and the modern philosophers of language there is a difference in their formulation of the problem. For the modern philosophers of language the problem is how the limitless understanding is generated by the limited rules of vocabulary and syntax ? For Bhartṛhari the basic question is: " how does our language function in limitless ways along with the variations in the rules of syntax and vocabulary ?" For him the rules of syntax and vocabulary can be varying and they are formulated by the Grammarians for the purpose of articulate expression of the sense and meaning. But the power of the words to express meaning in multiple contexts is ultimately rooted in the very dispositional linguistic ability present within each conscious being. The questions of vocabulary and syntax comes only after this linguistic ability is manifested in form of audible noise. *Sphoṭa* is the basic ground of linguistic expressibility itself. It implies the limitless potentiality which is rather expressed in limited and varying rules of syntax and vocabulary. So Bhartṛhari would rather consider what the modern philosophers call the 'rules of syntax and vocabulary' a part of our very linguistic potency. They do not precede our understanding of 'language' as a concept, rather the rules are the results of our capability to present our thought in a meaningful way. So he says that the real linguistic potency is in our inner faculty of intellect (*buddhi*) — all the differentiations, including the differentiations of the grammar and syntax are due to its presentation in the forms of audible noise, (*śabdo'pi buddhisthita śrutiṇām kāraṇam pṛthak*).[16] The concept of *sphoṭa* is considered to be non-differentiated. But when expressed in language it not only varies according to the variations in the speaker's way of saying, but also according to the regional usages prevalent in different parts of the world. The rules of grammar and syntax vary from language to language. But such variations do not affect the very basis of 'language', as the ultimate ground of words and meanings. Bhartṛhari's solution to the basic problem raised above may not sound very appealing to the modern philosophers of language. But their way of solving the issue has so far been not very satisfactory. Some of them have sought a solution by laying bare structural principles of our limitless linguistic understanding by an appeal to the formal logic. So they take resort to an analysis of truth-conditions, reference, predication. etc. If Bhartṛhari's metaphysical basis is Monistic, then the Western philosophy of language is rooted in the metaphysics of dualism. In other words their way of looking at language is always determined by the fundamental distinction between the particulars and the concepts, the reference and predication, the 'that' of the subject and the 'what' of the predicate. So the Western philosophy of language is inextricably related with the problem of 'truth' and truth-conditionality. The concepts of 'reference' and 'predication' are epistemological. But when these two concepts form the very basis and structural ground of all sorts of analysis of linguistic principles, then automatically they are raised to the status of the metaphysical principles. At the same time we must take care to notice that the modern version of the metaphysics of language is a form of descriptive metaphysics, for it abstracts the ultimate principles of language from the very nature of the general pattern of discourse. But Bhartṛhari's is revisionary metaphysics, because his world-view as well as the general view of language is largely influenced by his conceptual preference for the 'non-difference' and 'unity'.

Let us now come back to the issue we had taken up earlier, i.e., what is the role of *sphoṭa* in explaining the nature of language ? I have already stated the importance of the concept of *sphoṭa* in explaining the puzzle about the limitless ways of linguistic understanding. Now, we will pay attention to another, equally perplexing problem of philosophy of language. We all know that language is a means of communication. In case of linguistic communication the speaker is the person who expresses what he intends to say and the hearer is the person who is supposed to understand what the speaker means to say. Unless the hearer grasps the 'meaning conveyed' by the speaker, the communication fails. But the moot question is — how does the speaker transfer the meaning to the hearer ? The obvious answer to this question seems to be that it is because both, the speaker and the hearer, share the same linguistic convention. But the problem raised here is not that simple that it can be solved by as simple an answer. Bhartṛhari, atleast, would not accept the answer offered as good enough. Following him we can reformulate the problem again. How do we explain the case of the gaps in communication in spite of the speaker and the hearer 'sharing' the common linguistic rules ? The hearer may be attentive and may hear carefully the utterances made by the speaker, yet there are times when he fails to grasp what the speaker means. How such gaps in linguistic communication arise ? Bhartṛhari would say that such an issue is unanswerable as long as we think that the meaning is directly transferred from one person to another. To put it in a somewhat modern way, the meanings are not objects that can be transferred from one place to another place as we load the contents of one car into another car. The ability to express in speech-form, as well as the ability to discern meaning, both, are the two dimensions of the linguistic potency possessed by all conscious beings. This potency is otherwise known as *śabda* or *sphoṭa*. The fundamental idea is that both, the expressive word and the meaning expressed are present in the consciousness of the speaker and the hearer. In other words the hearer and the speaker share the same *sphoṭa* (which by no means is equivalent to a set of the rules of syntax and convention of a language). When the speaker desires to say something he grasps the unit of meaning first and then expresses it in sequential form of utterance, syllable by syllable. The hearer on the other hand, grasps the sequential and audible words first and these words evoke his 'linguistic potency' and through it he understands what the speaker intends to say. This awakening of the hearer's *sphoṭa* causes the comprehension by the hearer of the sentence uttered. Thus the process of communicability can be seen from two standpoints, the speaker's and the hearer's. From the speaker's standpoint prior to the utterance of a meaningful statement the idea of what he intends to say is within him in non-sequential and undifferentiated form. It is this potency which makes it possible for him to express his intention in the form of utterance. So from the speaker's standpoint the linguistic potency or the principle of language is the cause (*nimitta*) of the uttered sounds. But from the hearer's standpoint the utterance by the speaker allows the hearer to refer to his potency to understand meaning (*pratyāyaka*). In this sense the spoken words are the cause of understanding of the meaning. Therefore in the process of linguistic communication both the speaker and the hearer have to use their potential linguistic power, which, as we have seen, implies both — the power to use audible word forms and the power to convey meaning. And this is what is meant by the 'sharing of the same *sphoṭa*' by the speaker and the hearer. To express it in Bhartṛhari's way: "The potency of language is like a pea-hen's egg. All the colours of a fully grown pea-hen is potentially there in the egg. These colours are manifested when the pea-hen comes out of the egg. Similarly the *sphoṭa* or *śabda* is the potential stage in which the linguistic forms along with its power to mean is already present in all 'languageing' being.[17] This is Bhartṛhari's explanation regarding the problem of transferability of meaning from the speaker to the hearer.

So far we were discussing how Bhartṛhari's concept of *sphoṭa* can be useful in solving some crucial problems of the philosophy of language. Now we will go further to examine the various implications of this concept. But before we do so, we must clear one confusion that arises from Bhartṛhari's explanations about the nature of *sphoṭa.* Sometimes it appears from his statements that when we express our thoughts in language, the *sphoṭa* itself is manifested in the forms of units of meaning. In verse I.48 he says:

> Since *nāda* (sound) arises in sequence, *sphoṭa* which has neither a former nor a latter stage and which is sequenceless (*akrama*) is apprehended (through *nāda*) and appears to be having sequence as well as parts.

Then in the next verse he says :

> (Thus properties of *nāda* are transferred to *sphoṭa*) the reflected image (of the moon for example) although it resides in a separate location, seems to share the operation (the movement of the waves in the water) of objects in a separate location; *sphoṭa* being manifested in the *nāda* in the same way.

The above passage imply that he not only means by *sphoṭa* the unitary and undifferentiated ground of word and meaning, but also the unit of meaning conveyed by the speaker to mean particular episodes, events, or things. But all along he mentions that these expressed units of meaning are impermanent and unreal (like the movement of moon in the flowing water). Besides, in the previous chapter we have seen that according to him the 'language' as a principle implies the **whole** which is expressed for communicative purposes in 'bits' and 'parts'. So we may solve this apparent confusion by making a distinction between the meaning of *sphoṭa* as the very potency for linguistic expressibility and understanding, which is there in human inner faculty (*buddhi*) or the intellect; and the meaning of *sphoṭa* as the unit of meaning expressed by each meaningful utterance. If we accept that the true significance of the term is only the latter one, then there will be innumerable *sphoṭas*, not one. This will be very much inconsistent with Bhartṛhari's entire philosophical outlook. So in all probability he used the term *sphoṭa* or *śabda* in extended sense when he talks of *sphoṭa* in the context of **words** and **sentences**. He used the term *sphoṭa* in extended sense to signify **any** unit of meaning. This is obvious from the fact that he also talks of *varṇa* (phoneme) *sphoṭa*, *pada* (word) *sphoṭa* and *vākya* (sentence) *sphoṭa*. At the same time in the second *Kāṇḍa* of *Vākyapadīya* he offers a series of justifications to show that it is the **sentence**, not the word and phoneme, which is the primary unit of meaning. He rather says that for grammatical and practical purposes we make an artificial division amongst phonemes, words and so on. For a proper understanding of the nature of language, he shows that we can abstract phonemes from words, words from sentences, sentences from passages and passages from still bigger passages and so on. This method of analysis is known as *apoddhāra*. Still some snags seem to remain in his theory. Why does he insist so much on the primary of *vākya sphoṭa* ? Does he mean by *sphoṭa* the 'sense' conveyed by the sentence on different occasions as the funamental basis of his language analysis ? It is obvious that he offers primacy to the 'meaning' expressed by a sentence and calls them *sphoṭa* because he in such cases refers to 'language-in-use', not 'language-in-principle'. At the level of linguistic usage the primary unit of meaning can only be located in sentences, not in words. As he is more interested in 'sense' than 'reference' sentences for him represent the primary linguistic unit. But while talking of the structural element of language as a whole, he introduces the notion of *sphoṭa* as the potential ground for the whole range of elements associated with the linguistic communication. It is made clear in his commentary on verse I.56:

> The external (audible) word employed in verbal usage, is merged in the mind after suppressing all assumptions of differentation, without, however, abandoning the residual force of differentiation, as in the case of the yolk of the pea-hen. Just as one single word can merge, so can passages consisting of as many as ten parts. The word, thus merged, with all differentiation suppressed, again assumes differentiation and sequences, when through speaker's desire to say something, the inner word (*sphoṭa*) is awakened and **it becomes the sentence**

> **or the word**, each with its division. It is this merging and emerging of word which is looked upon as its activity.

This passage clearly shows that though at places Bhartṛhari talks of *sphoṭa* being manifested in particular sentences or words, and though he talks of *varṇa sphoṭa*, *pada sphoṭa* and *vākya sphoṭa*, the term has a different significance when he talks of *sphoṭa* as the ultimate ground of linguistic manifestations.

Bhartṛhari on Speaker's Communication of Meaning

We have already noted that Bhartṛhari's concept of *sphoṭa* can serve as the logical ground for the communication between the speaker and the hearer. We must now focus our attention to the process of communication, as it is conceived by Bhartṛhari. We know quite well that for linguistic communication to be possible the speaker must express his intention and the hearer must understand what the speaker intends to mean. We have also seen that the process of communication cannot be understood if we keep our investigation only limited to the area of uttered speech. We have to go beyond the level of utterance to explain how language is comprehended.

Bhartṛhari conceives of three stages of linguistic expressibility — the *paśyantī*, *madhyamā* and *vaikhārī*. *Paśyantī* is the latent stage of language. At this stage the distinction between the word-forms and meanings are not there. Following Matilal[18] I will prefer to translate the *paśyantī* as non-verbal stage. *Madhyamā* is the intermediate stage, where despite the indentity of thought and language their distinction along with the distinctive elements of words and meanings are discernible. This stage is the 'pre-verbal' stage. And *vaikhārī* is the 'verbal' stage, i.e., when the language is presented in audible form along with the elements of accent, pitch, meaning, etc. This is how the speaker's potential linguistic ability works when he intends to say something. But how does the hearer comprehend it ? We have seen, that according to Bhartṛhari the spoken words do not directly transfer the meaning to the hearer. It only awakens the hearer's linguistic potency, which in turn, leads him to the comprehension of meaning. Such an explanation of hearer's linguistic comprehension may seem very peculiar. Why this round-about way, when the hearer can directly draw the meaning from the speaker's utterance ? This is because, Bhartṛhari and other Indian Philosophers take very seriously the sequential nature of the utterance. The utterance is expressed syllable by syllable, part by part but ultimately it conveys a unitary meaning. So their problem is: how does the hearer comprehend and the speaker convey the unitary meaning out of the particularised series of sound-patterns ? And this shows why Bhartṛhari does not believe that meaning of a linguistic expression can be directly conveyed to the hearer through the merging and emerging sequences of phonetic elements.

Now let us see how Bhartṛhari handles this problem of sequential syllables and non-sequential and unitary sense or meaning of the uttered words. Bhartṛhari's problem is to show at what stage of utterance, the meaning as a unit is conveyed. Let us analyse his problem with an example. If X utters the word 'cow' — he has to express it vocally as 'C' 'O' 'W'. Here, there are three sound units, which taken together implies, 'Cow' as a meaningful element. Bhartṛhari believes that each letter serves as a medium of manifestation of the unit of meaning 'cow'. Now, if the unity of meaning in this series of three letters 'C' 'O' 'W' is manifested from the beginning by the first sound-unit then there is unnecessary repetition and redundancy. If it is the last sound-unit which is responsible for cognition of the unitary meaning, then the preceding sound-units are superfluous. Besides, by the time somebody utters the last sound-unit the preceding sound-units are no more heard. Bhartṛhari avoids the problem of repetitiveness, by postulating that each sound-unit results in a distinctive property (*viśeṣa*) in the level of awareness or comprehension. So the first syllablle 'C' expresses the whole unit of meaning but in a indistinct way. It becomes progressively clear with the utterance of successive sound-units till the last sound-unit is uttered.[19] By the time the last sound-unit is uttered, the preceding sound-units have disappeared. But the memory impressions of the preceding sound-units are retained. So these memory-impressions along with the hearing of the last syllable gives the hearer the total unit of meaning. However, Bhartṛhari's account of the comprehension of meaning-units may seem to be unsatisfactory. If the whole meaning of the word 'cow' is expressed by each individual syllable 'C' 'O' 'W', then one can comprehend 'cow' from the utterance of each syllable. But the hearer perceives each individual syllable separately. And the unit of total meaning is not identical with individual syllables. Bhartṛhari answers this objection with the help of *Vaiśeṣika* theory of numbers. He says, just as the cognition, of lower numbers 'one' or 'two' is a means for cognising the higher numbers, like 'three', similarly the comprehension of the units of meaning (be it of the word or sentence), is conditioned by the cognition of the constituent sound-units. According to the *Vaiśeṣika* theory of numbers, each number is distinct from another number. And all numbers higher than the preceding numbers are produced by a sort of "connective-comparative" cognition, which is called *apekṣābuddhi.*[20] This is the notion through which many unities are brought under one number or another. When two things are cognised, one cognises them as "this is one and that is one". This gives rise to the cognition of 'two' or duality. And in this process each succeeding number is cognised. According to this theory, cognition of the previous number is the condition for cognising the succeeding numbers. Applying the same logic of the comprehension of numbers Bhartṛhari argues that understanding and awareness of the distinct sound elements is the means for cognition of the combined unity of the meaning. If the speaker wants to convey the meaning to the hearer he has to take recourse to the unavoidable and essential condition of presenting his thought through sequential elements of sound-units (*nāda*). One has to take cognisance of this peculiar characteristic of language. Bhartṛhari, also compares the hearer's understanding of language with the process of painting. The painter while painting, say, a landscape perceives his object of painting in parts, then he visualises the whole and then while painting on a canvas he paints it part by part. Simillarly, the hearer cognises the speaker's words part by part and then grasps the whole meaning; and again, while responding to the speaker's statements, he expresses his thought part by part.

Hearer's Understandsing and *Pratibhā*

Bhartṛhari, we now see, has offered his own explanation about the hearer's comprehension of the unitary meaning from the sequential presentation of the speaker's thought and intention. Still, one feels that the entire issue of hearer's comprehension of language is not resolved. The issue I raised sometime back regarding the gap in communication between the speaker and the hearer remains unresolved. We know of many instances, where the hearer in spite of listening to the whole statement fails to comprehend what it means.[21] The above explanation about the comprehension of meaning from sequential speech-pattern does not include this issue. But Bhartṛhari is not oblivious of the problem. He believes that the hearer does not comprehend the meaning directly from the speaker's utterance. So Bhartṛhari introduces another concept, called *pratibhā* to explain the problem of linguistic communication. *Pratibhā* very broadly signifies the *intuitive* linguistic disposition.

Pratibhā is a concept which cannot be defined. Bhartṛhari explains it in the following way:

> This *pratibhā* cannot be in any way explained to others in terms of "it is this", its existence can be ratified only in the individual's expreience of it, and the experiencer himself cannot describe it.[22]

This concept is very unique in the sense that, in no other system except *Yoga*, is such a concept brought in to explain the nature of linguistic meaning. Bhartṛhari and other *sphoṭa-vādins* take help of this concept to explain the hearer's understanding of meaning. The gap in communication arises when the hearer lacks this intuition.

We have noticed that the meaning is always expressed through the sequential *nāda*. The 'sense' or the meaning of a statement, however, is indivisible and integral unit. This can be grasped in an instantaneous flash or intuition. So the hearer understands the meaning as if in a flash. Puṇyarāja while interpreting the verse II.2. of *Vākyapadīya* says that the sentence-meaning is not built up gradually on the basis of word-meanings, it is grasped through instantaneous flash of insight. This understanding does not have parts and it is grasped by the mind. This in neither spatial nor particular, nor dependent on peculiarities of particular language. It is the instinctive power of the mind. *Pratibhā* can be experienced but cannot be expressed, because it is the very basis of understanding and linguistic experience. In this sense it is the *a-priori* condition of linguistic understanding.

Bhartṛhari, of course, uses the term in a very wide and comprehensive sense, so as to include the instinctive nature of the animal as well as the special intuitive power of the *yogīs*. He believes that even the birds and animals have this instinctive power to express themselves, though their communicative process is not as articulate as men. Such an interpretation may lead us to the controversial question, whether animal language is possible or not ? But this is not our concern here. What we must concentrate on is : what does *pratibhā* as a concept has any significance ? It may be very easy on our part to dismiss off this idea as a sort of mystical explanation, having nothing do with philosophy of language. There are also plenty of grounds available for doing so. Bhartṛhari himself says that this concept cannot be stated in the form of a definition. It cannot be even described by the individual who experiences it. Besides, Bhartṛhari says that our instantaneous intuition of linguistic understanding draws its support from the knowledge of words acquired through previous birth (*saṁskāra*). So let us now see how much of his theory is mystical and how much of it conforms to the structural conditions of linguistic understanding.

I shall start by taking the issue of *saṁskāra*, i.e., the linguistic disposition acquired from the previous birth. This notion is no doubt unscientific. What Bhartṛhari intended to prove is that our linguistic ability is not totally dependent on learning the rules of language, i.e., convention and syntax. The human ability to express himself is innate (in the sense, that it is a part of the human nature). The rules of language and convention make it articulate. Without this, what one intends to say may not be properly conveyed. But man's ability to apply these rules in unlimited number of ways is not dependent on such rules themselves. This phenomenon has always perplexed the philosophers and it continues to do so. Bhartṛhari finds an answer to this perplexing issue with the help of the traditional belief of his time. In Indian cultural tradition, especially the orthodox tradition, the belief in immortality of soul as well as in rebirth were uniformly accepted. So we cannot exactly blame him for referring to previous birth. Nobody can deny the fact that the philosophical understanding of every age is determined by the progress of knowledge made during the time. As Galileo could not have talked of in terms of neutrons and protons, similarly the ancient linguists could not have talked in terms of 'disposition', 'linguistic zone' of brain, etc.

Wittgenstein on Understanding

Now we come to the issue of 'intuitive' knowledge or 'instantaneous flash of understanding'. Most of the modern scholars of philosophy will shrink to use the term 'intuition'. It is generally believed that if we are talking of cognition, knowledge, or language, then we must talk either in terms of 'experience' or in terms of the 'rules of logic' and 'syntax'. The knowledge derived from experience is verifiable, hence meaningful. The knowledge derived from the 'rules of logic' are meaningful because they do not inform but offer us rules of inference. So the term 'intuition' is considered to be unscientific, uncritical, primitive and sometimes mystical. Yet it is a matter of experience, especially in case of our understanding that we do take help of intuition. Sometimes even after several attempts, meanings of certain passages, certain discourses remain vague to us. And then in a sudden flash of intuition we grasp the meaning. In science, in mathematics, in poetics the role of 'intuitive' knowledge is already acclaimed. Bhartṛhari, however talks of intuitive knowledge in all cases of grasping the meaning because he finds the riddle of sequential nature of understanding quite perplexing. This riddle does not figure at all in modern philosophy of language. But no philosopher of language can deny their puzzlements about the human ability to understand unlimited ways of linguistic usage. No philosopher can give a proper explanation of what constitutes the linguistic disposition, except postulating that there is such a power or disposition to use language or understand language in unlimited number of ways. If we take these facts into consideration then it seems there is nothing mystical about Bhartṛhari's postulation of *pratibhā* as the intuitive faculty of operating with language. Before winding up our discussion on Bhartṛhari's notion of *sphoṭa* and communicative meaning I want to draw the reader's attention to a very interesting yet radically different interpretation of the concept of 'intuitive' understanding. This is offered by Wittgenstein. We have seen that Bhartṛhari introduces the notion of intuitive flash or *pratibhā* to explain hearer's understanding. This problem also bothers Wittgenstein. In his book *Philosophical Investigations*, he emphasises the communicative role of language. Therefore the idea of hearer's understanding does not escape his notice, during his post-*Tractatus* phase. He says :

> It seems there are **certain definite** mental processes bound up with the workings of language, processes through which alone language can function. I mean the processes of understanding and meaning. The signs of our language seem dead without these mental processes: and it might seem that the only function of sign is to induce such processes, and that these are the things we ought really to be interested in.[23]

But this interest in mental processes seems to go against his anti-mentalistic stand of *Philosophical Investigations.* Here, he takes resort to a form of linguistic behaviourism which allows no scope for understanding the mental processes. He dismisses the role of any such intermediary step between the actual level of utterance and the hearer's understanding. There is no need to think, he says, that the hearer must be engaged in a mental act before he responds to the speaker's utterance. This intermediary step of mental states is considered to be a 'grammatical fiction'. In short, there are no such mental states occurring privately in speaker's or hearer's mind. Neither 'meaning', nor 'understanding' is the name of any such mental process. We say such things as, "Since he understood what I said, he did the right thing"; or "Because he understood the principles involved, he was able to solve the problem". Embodied in these and other ways of talking is the picture of a person's (processes of) 'understanding' as mental cause of his overt behaviour, as a mental reservoir from which action flows. This is a sort of picture thinking and the manifestation of a "general disease of thinking." (*Blue and Brown Book*, p. 143)

He offers many examples of the cases when we clearly believe that intuitive flash is at work.[24] When 'X' is given a sequence of numbers and asked to continue the series, he may be said to have an intuitive understanding about how to proceed. Again everyone has the experience of understanding certain things 'in a flash'. He discusses such examples and makes an effort to show that there are no such mental states. But, what then is 'understandings' ? Wittgenstein would refuse to answer such question. For 'meaning', 'understanding' and other such words are not definable, as they have no common essence. "Once we have an overall view of the variety of situations in which the terms 'meaning' and 'understanding' are used, and of the various cariteria of their use, there is nothing more to know about what meaning and understanding are. To know their use, Wittgnstein would say, is to know their meaning".[25] He at the same time admits, that words get their life by being used in communication. The speaker must mean something by his utterance and the hearer must understand what he means. But the terms 'intention' and 'understanding' signify nothing more than observing how and when such words are used. He is not willing to budge an inch beyond the level of utterance, even though he admits that language implies communication.

In case of Bhartṛhari, we have noticed, there is no such hesitation about explaining the questions of speaker's 'intention' and hearer's 'understanding' in terms of pre-linguistic mental states. He does not want to reduce the entire phenomena of language-in-use to the process of verbalisation. It is very difficult to say which one is the correct account of meaning and language. It all depends on how they (Bhartṛhari and Wittgenstein) look at the concept of 'language' itself.

References

1. Matilal, *Word and World*, p. 77.
2. A.B. Keith, *A History of Sanskrit Literature*, Oxford: Oxford University Press, 1928, p. 387.
3. S.K. De, *Studies In the History of Indian Poetics*, London: Luzac and Co., 1925, p. 180.
4. Pāṇini, *Aṣṭādhyāyī*, 6.1.123.
5. Haradatta, *Padamañjarī*, Under Pāṇini's above rule.
6. Yāska, *Nirukta*, 1.1.
7. John Brough, "Theories of General Linguistics in the Sanskrit Grammarians", In *Transactions of Philosophical Society*, 1951, 27-46 (34).
8. Patañjali under Pāṇini's rule, 1.1.70.
9. Brough, 'Theories of General Linguistics', p. 34.
10. K.K. Raja, *Indian Theories of Meaning*, Madras : Adyar Library, 1969, pp. 97-148.
11. S.D. Joshi, *The Sphoṭa nirṇaya of Kaunda Bhaṭṭa*, Poona, 1967, p. 40.
12. G. Caradona, *Pāṇini : A Survey of Research,* The Hague: Mouten and Co., 1976, p. 302.
13. K.A.S. Iyer, *Bhartṛhari*, pp. 158-59.
14. Matilal, *Word and World*, p. 85.
15. P.F. Strawson, "Meaning and Understanding", In *Analysis and Metaphysics*, p. 98.
16. *Vākyapadīya*, I.46.
17. *Vākyapadīya, Vṛtti* Under 1-58, tr. by Iyer.
18. Matilal, *Word and World*, p. 88.
19. *Vākyapadīya*, I.83-84.
20. *Ibid.*, p. 92. also *Vāk.* I.87, and *Vṛtti* under the verse.

21. *Rg Veda*, 10-71 offers a very insightful remark about the nature of language. The verse says: "Many who look do not see, many who listen do not hear it. It reveals itself like a loving and well-adorned wife to her husband".
22. *Vāk*, III.146.
23. L. Wittgenstein, *The Blue and Brown Books*, Oxford: Basil and Blackwell, p. 3. *See* also *Philosophical Investigations*, Section 358.
24. Wittgenstein, *P.I.*, Sections 210-14, 138, 139, 151, 155, 179, 180.
25. George Pitcher, *The Philosophy of Wittgenstein*, Delhi: Prentice Hall of India Pvt. Ltd., 1977, p. 275.

4

The Word and the Meaning

Nature of the Relationship

WE all know that human beings take recourse to language to mean something. That 'something' may be an event, an object, an emotion, a command or a question, etc. But without the use of words these varied sorts of phenomena included within the name 'meaning' are not expressible. Most often common man as well as philosophers forget about the importance of words and concentrate on meaning. But to have a comprehensive knowledge about how language functions one must probe into the nature of relation between the word and meaning. For, this is the very basis of exploring the nature and function of language. However, at the outset, I must make it clear that the term 'word' is not used here in a literal sense. By 'word' I mean the linguistic expression as a whole.

While discussing Bhartṛhari's theory of *sphoṭa* we have seen that the concept symbolises an identity between two diverse linguistic elements, viz., the forms of words and the meaning. We have also noted that forms of words do not imply just the phonetic act of producing audible sounds, but sounds with a particular form and order. In this chapter our primary concern is to investigate how Bhartṛhari relates these diverse elements; viz., words and meaning. It should be kept in mind that the words themselves are not meanings, but they express the meaning. In Bhartṛhari's language the form of word is the conveyor or the expression, i.e., *vācaka*, and that which is conveyed or expressed is the meaning, i.e., *vācya*. When the speaker intends to say something, he has to take care of these two aspects of language. He has to express in appropriate form of words and the exact meaning that he wants to convey. Before translating his thought into audible form both the elements, i.e., the form of words and meaning are present in potential form in his *buddhi* (the inner faculty or consciousness). Though these two elements stem from the same source, i.e., the *sphoṭa*, at the pre-verbal stage they are differentiated and distinguished. This is what Bhartṛhari means when he says that the first differentiation of linguistic potency occurs in the realm of *buddhi*.[1] Such differentiation is needed when the speaker becomes conscious that he has to communicate a particular thought or idea. But the words have not yet become audible nor the meaning is conveyed. The particular *vācya* (the contents of meaning) and *vācaka* (the word-forms) are grasped by the speaker before he starts making utterances.[2] The hearer also grasps these two elements before deciphering what the speaker intends by his utterance. We often tend to neglect the role of the *vācaka*. But one may notice that when the word-forms are not properly grasped, by the hearer, he is likely to ask : "what did you say?".[3] So both the *vācya* and *vācaka* play equally prominent roles in linguistic communication. Bhartṛhari, in broad sense, calls the *vācya* as *artha* (meaning) and the *vācaka* as *śabda* (words).[4] He also views the *vācaka* as *śrutiśakti* (the power of being heard) and *vācya* as *arthaśakti* (the power of being meaningful).[5] He also designates them as *prakāśatvam* (illuminator) and *prakāśyatvam* (illuminated).[6]

Bhartṛhari also points out another peculiar feature of language. In other forms of cognition, say, perception — the instrument of perception is not itself perceivable. We see things with eyes, but our eye itself is not visible. In case of cognition by linguistic means the instrument of such cognition, i.e., the word, itself is cognisable. In fact we cannot cognise linguistic facts without cognising the medium of cognition (words) first.[7] Therefore linguistic cognition is a special type of cognition. Our language is endowed with two powers, the power of revealing the meaning (*grāhaka*) and that of revealing itself (*grāhakatva*).[8]

Thus far we have seen that Bhartṛhari offers equal significance to words and meaning. Now Bhartṛhari's probelm is to explain how these two distinct linguistic elements are related. In the III part of *Vākyapadīya* he devotes one whole section to investigate and explain the concept of 'relationship' with specific reference to word and meaning. He envisages this relationship as two-fold in nature.

The word and meaning are bound by the relationship of inherent and natural fitness (*yogyatā*) and also by the relationship of causality (*kārya-kāraṇa bhāva*).[9] Sometimes he also uses the latter relation to explain the link between the form of words and the speaker's intention. To explicate the nature of relationship in greater detail, he identifies three elements in case of an utterance. They are : (1) the own form of words, (2) the meaning, (in certain sense it also includes the object-meant), and (3) the speaker's intention.[10] He views the relationship between the phonetic act of utterance and the form of words as the most intimate one (*antaraṅga*).[11] This is called intimate because the hearer along with hearing the audible sounds also comes in contact with the forms of words. This is the initial means of grasping the word-forms. While the relation between the word-forms and meaning is called *vācya-vācaka bhāva*, the relation between the word and the intention of the speaker is called *kārya-kāraṇa bhāva*. Sometimes Bhartṛhari also applies *kārya-kāraṇa bhāva* to explain the relation between the word and meaning. The relationship is called *vācya-vācaka bhāva*, because the word is the conveyor and the meaning is what is conveyed. From another standpoint it is the word which causes the grasping of meaning in the hearer. So it is also described in terms of causality (*kārya-kāraṇa bhāva*).[12]

Both these dimensions of word-meaning relationship stem from a natural fitness (*yogyatā*) of words to express meaning. This power of conveying the meaning is inherent in the words. It is 'natural' because it is not created at a particular moment of time by any body.[13] It is not a case of human decision to use words for expressing meaning. Human beings cannot and has not created this relation. Man only knows that he uses words to express meaning. And he learns to use particular words to express particular meaning by watching the elders.[14] It is a matter convention when it comes to the level of particular linguistic usage. The convention (*saṁketa* or *samaya*) can be made in two ways. Some words are used to express certain meanings since time immemorial, but certain words can be specifically coined from time-to-time for use in special and technical sciences.

However, when it comes to the relationship between the word and their expressive power the relationship is to be considered as 'eternal' (*nitya*).[15] There should not be any misgivings about the use of the word 'eternal'. Bhartṛhari himself makes it clear. He says that the term 'eternal' can have two meanings. Something which has no beginning or end, something unchangeable is called 'eternal'. But it is eternal in absolute sense (*kūṭastha nityatā*). Bhartṛhari's conception of *śabda Brahman* conforms to this sort of use. Again 'eternity' may be used in the sense of 'continuity'. In this sense it is applied in case of word-meaning relationship. The words that are used as sound-token in particular linguistic utterances disappear once they are uttered. Yet we recognise such words along with their meaning in a thousand cases of utterances with all variations in account and pitch. Again, the words continue to express the same meaning, though they are used in different contexts. The word 'jar' means a particular 'jar' though it can be used to refer to different individual jars. Such continuity and uniformity of meaning amidst variations and changes is also a form of 'eternity', according to Bhartṛhari. He calls this *pravāhanityatā*, [16] i.e., the continuity amidst the stream of change. In this sense, *yogyatā*, the inherent fitness of words, to express meaning is eternal. The linguistic communication is made possible only on the basis of such continuity of relation between the word and meaning.

We can express the relation between the word and meaning through two types of statements. Either we say "this expressive power belongs to that (words)" or we can state it as "it (word) is that (expressive power)".[17] In the first way of putting things, a distinction is made between the word and meaning. In the latter case the identity between the word and meaning is emphasised. The former way of looking at the relationship is helpful in case of grammar and lexicography. But Bhartṛhari prefers the latter way of describing the relationship, i.e., the relation of identity. It is more appropriate for understanding the communicative role of meaning, in case of language-in-use.

Bhartṛhari also views the word-meaning relationship in terms of causality (*kārya-kāraṇa bhāva*). In this connection we must examine his notion of *samjñā* and *samjñīn*.[18] It is sometimes translated as 'name' and 'named'. It is usually believed that word as *samjñā* is used to signify some object or event external to our mind. When we use the word 'jar' it is supposed to stand for the object 'jar'. In this sense, word and the object-meant have a relation of 'designate and designated'. But Bhartṛhari does not understand the relation between *samjñā* and *samjñīn* in this sense. For him, both belong to the realm of language. No doubt, we use words to designate objects. But all 'objects' meant are not externally existent. There are words like "wheel of fire", "barren woman's son" etc., which has no corresponding external object. Similarly, in case of negative statement 'the tree does not exist' there cannot be an external event corresponding to 'non-existence'. We may add to the list many such forms of expression, which do not designate any external event. So the object-named does not necessarily imply existent objects. These cases lend support to Bhartṛhari's theory that *saṃjñā* does not directly mean 'objects', but concepts or 'thought-objects'.[19] Both belong to the level of linguistic cognition. Understood in this sense, the relation between the word and meaning can be viewed as causal. It is the word which brings to the mind of the hearer the 'idea of the object'. Again in case of the speaker the 'idea of the object' causes the use as well as the choice of appropriate words.

If the words do not refer to objects and meaning is not referential then what do the words, 'mean'? We usually believe that the words always mean a particular object or fact. Since in Bhartṛhari's scheme of analysis there is scope for direct reference, we are left with words without anything being 'named' or 'meant'. But we have seen that according to Bhartṛhari words mean concepts or 'thought-objects'. They are linguistic entities, not objective entities. Such entities are bound to be universal. But what about the utterances where we use words to mean a particular? When I say 'this rose is red', I do not mean by 'rose' the universal class of 'rose' but a particular rose. Bhartṛhari's answer to this problem is that a word can denote individuals indirectly. This is done on the basis of a universal which belongs to the word itself. He would say the particular 'rose' is referred to on the basis of our knowledge of the universal character of 'rose-ness'. Bhartṛhari sorts out two opposing views regarding the issue of meaning and referent. One is ascribed to *Vyādi* and the other to *Vyājapāyana. Vyādi* regards the individuals as the proper referent, while the latter regards universals as constituting the referent. In other words one regards individuals as the object-meant and the other offers this status to the universals. Helārāja, the commentator on Bhartṛhari's part III of *Vākyapadīya*, adds a third view.[20] According to this view the individual characterised or qualified by the universal constitutes the meaning of a word. However Bhartṛhari asserts that all words first of all mean or designate the universal and this is superimposed on the particular of the objective world. If we accept this view, then a subtle philosophical question may be raised. What is this 'universal' that we mean by words ? Does the universal belong to the realm of existence or to the realm of words ? It is believed by some philosophers that the universal is not simply a mental or linguistic category. It is real and existent in the objects of the world. The rose is called 'rose' because it shares the essence of 'roseness' existing objectively. But Bhartṛhari does not subscribe to such a view. For him the universals are linguistic constructs (*vikalpa*) and universals are primarily 'word-universals' transformed into 'thing-universals' for facilitating our utterances about the world and things.[21]

So far we have been discussing the first two elements of a linguistic utterance, i.e., word and the meaning. Now let us do a brief scanning of third element, i.e., the speaker's intention. Full credit must be given to Bhartṛhari for bringing the 'speaker's intention' within the scope of philosophy of language. In Indian philosophy there are elaborate discussions on the concept of 'intended meaning' or 'contextual meaning'. Therefore some interpreters claim that analysis of 'intention' has been a part of philosophical discussions on language in most of the philosophical traditions. Here, I beg to differ from such an interpretation. Such an interpretation is based on the translation of the word *tātparya* as 'intention'. Some Indian philosophical Schools conceive that a sentence in order to be comprehended as meaningful unit must be characterised by four factors. They are *ākāṅkṣā* (syntactic expectancy), *yogyatā* (logical consistency) *sannidhi* (phonetic contiguity) and *tātparya* (the contextual factors). The last element, i.e., *tātparya* was a later addition made by *Nyāya* School. As an example of *tātparya*, most often, the case of *saindhava* is stated. The word *saindhava* has two meanings, viz. salt and horse. If somebody says "Bring *saindhava*". How is the hearer going to comprehend the meaning ? If the statement is uttered while eating, the context demands that *saindhava* should mean 'salt' not horse. So *tātparya* is connected with hearer's comprehension of the intended meaning. But while uttering the sentence the speaker also expresses his intention. There is definitely a difference between the **speaker's intention** in saying something, and the hearer's **comprehension** of the speakers intention. *Tātparya* stands for the contextual meaning to be comprehended by the hearer. Bhartṛhari also provides a very insightful account of *tātparya*. But this should not be confused with the speaker's intention. For he uses a different word to signify it. It is called the *abhiprāya* of the *vaktā*.[22] In the Western philosophy of language, Grice, Austin and Searle have highlighted on the factor of speaker's intention. Rather they have over-emphasized it, for their analysis of meaning is more or less speaker-oriented. On the other hand the classical Indian thinkers placed more emphasis on the hearer's comprehension. But in Bhartṛhari's account of language, a balance is achieved between these two ways of looking at the problem of meaning.

According to Bhartṛhari there is a relationship between the words and the speaker's intention. It is a relationship of causality. It is the speaker's intention to communicate, which initiates his speech. In other words he expresses himself through spoken words because he has the urge to communicate. So intention of the speaker is the cause of uttered words. On the other hand, the utterances arouse in the hearer the need to understand what the speaker intends. Therefore, there is a relationship of cause and effect between the elements of word-forms and speaker's intention. In this sense, the intention of the speaker is a part of the network of factors that help us to understand the notion of linguistic communicability.

What does the Word Mean ? Some Western Theories

So far we have been concentrating primarily on Bhartṛhari's notion of word-meaning relationship. Now for a while, let us shift our attention to another way of dealing with the issue. An in-depth probe into the Western philosophy of language reveals that their basic concern is not understanding the exact nature of relationship between the word and the meaning. Rather there is a clear attempt to unravel what the words should mean in order to be significant. In other words their primary concern is locating a criterion for meaning. We cannot avoid examination of this issue, as it forms a part of understanding the nature of language. Besides, our discussions on the topic may provide us with some insight for a better assessment of Bhartṛhari's views.

In the Western philosophy, the problem of meaning has been discussed from two different angles. There are some philosophers who have preferred to handle the concept of meaning in an abstract way. 'Meaning' as a concept is isolated from the level of its concrete realm of use. On the other hand, others have explored the significance of the concept 'meaning' from the functional standpoint, i.e., the level of actual linguistic transaction. Those who consider the former method as more suitable, treat the term 'meaning' as an abstract concept. It is something like geometrical concepts, such as, 'triangle' or 'circle'. In case of abstract concepts a suitable definition is fixed and then any idea suiting the definition is included within the concept. For example, we define the geometrical concept 'triangle' as a three-sided bound figure, whose sum of angles is equal to 180. Any figure that conforms to the 'essences' of triangle is called a 'triangle'. Similarly, some philosophers conceive that we can lay down the defining characteristic of 'meaning' and anything that conforms to it is called 'meaningful'. In other words, it is believed that we can fix the criterion of meaning by determining its essential characteristics. Wittgenstein in his later philosophy branded such approach to the problem of meaning as 'Essentialistic' approach. It is a model-oriented approach, characterised by a craving for the unity of essence. The other approach, popularised by later Wittgenstein, handles the concept of meaning as the part of a function. It is the function of communicating with language. So this group of thinkers analyse 'meaning' at the level of its operation in the varied contexts of human life.

(a) Essentialism

The Essentialistic approach is backed by a typical craving of philosophers for unity and precision. They want to explain the particularities and temporalities of the universe with some neat conceptual framework. In case of meaning too, the craving for unity is expressed through their search for some uniform 'essence', i.e., an 'essence' that can serve as the principle of unity for the diversities of our linguistic expressions. These philosophers explain the concept of meaning with two basic presuppositions: (1) 'meaning' like other concepts is a class-name, which can be defined through the identification of some common characteristics, (2) the 'essence' of meaning must be epistemologically independent of the level of practice, i.e., the actual employment of meaningful utterances. For the sake of brevity let us put such theories under two groups.

(i) The Referential Model.
(Meaning defined in terms of referents).

(ii) The Ideational Model.
(Meaning defined in terms of ideas, psychological or logical ideas).

(i) Referential Theories : The Referential theorists envisages that meaning of a word consists of what it refers to. This way of defining meaning is based on a desire to understand how our language is connected with the things of the world. The temptation to connect language with the world stems from the fact that often we use the word to 'mean' or to ask question about the 'referents'. Taken at its surface value, the theory represents the common man's attitude to the problem of meaning. We learn language by being pointed out. Moreover, the forms of our language are such, that it leaves us with an impression that for every word there must be a physical counterpart. Therefore, the words must stand for something objective, i.e., a thing, a quality, an event or a person. In our language even the mental states are described in physical terms. We talk of big heart, narrow mind, stretching of imagination, etc. Whereas in fact, only the physical objects can be big or small, stretched or turned. This dominance of physicalism, to some extent, lends support to the view that meaning can be attached to the referents alone. It is a sort of entitative view of language, i.e., meanings stand for entities. St. Augustine, in his theory of meaning states that 'meaning' means what it stands for, i.e., an objective referent. But it was J.S. Mill who largely influenced the subsequent Referential Theorists. According to him the smallest unit of meaningful expression is a word. And the words function as names. As the names stand for a place or person similarly all words must stand for something denotative. We understand the meaning of the word 'Fido' because it stands for Fido the dog. But all words are not proper names like 'Fido'. Elucidating further, Mill argues that the words are names, but not proper names. The term 'name' has a broader implication, for Mill. It includes not only complex words and descriptive phrases but also adjectives. In short, any word that can stand as the subject or predicate of a proposition is a name. This denotationistic and Referential model offered by Mill strongly influenced some of the subsequent philosophers. Meinong was one of them. For him, meaningful words must have referents. And if the referents are not traceable in the world of existence, then they should be hooked to some 'subsistent' entities.

However, a new logical dimension to the Referential model was added by Russell and Early Wittgenstein. Russell with his Theory of Description shows that words cannot stand for objects, in the sense Mill means it. Even the definite descriptive phrases, which are supposed to be the most suitable candidate for being called meaningful on the ground of their referring to the singular object, do not always stand for objects. So Russell thinks that we need a logical analysis of language to explain the role of referents. Russell and Wittgenstein introduced a new method of explaining meaning by the method of analysing proposition into its simplest form. These simple or atomic proposition are not further analysable into propositions but to simple elements called 'logical proper names'. The concatenation of such names are propositions. The logical proper names correspond to the simplest elements of Reality called 'objects'. So it seems that Russell and Wittgenstein stick to the Referential model, but they only replace 'ordinary names' by 'logical proper names'. Such a logical explanation overcomes the problem of relating language with physical facts. Both, the language and the facts are explained in terms a common logical structure. The referents are neither physical nor ontologically determined. But in all sorts of Referential theory we note a sort of gap. In case of Mill it is the gap between words and objects. In case of Russell and Wittgenstein it is the gap between the logical picture of language and the ordinary language. The logical analysis offered by Russell is neat and rigorous, whereas the ordinary language is too diversified to be bound by such a neat logical picture. Russell was so much enamoured of the precision of his logical analysis that he conceived of replacing ordinary language by an 'Ideal Language'. Only in case of such ideal language can there be a fixed structural relationship between the language and the reality. But the problem of closing the gap between the logical picture of Referential theory and the actual nature of ordinary language that we use, cannot be solved by dismissing the validity of ordinary language. If the problem of meaning is to be analysed then we must take into account the concrete level of language-in-use. Neither the facts nor the language can be so pinpointed and so adjusted to have the one-to-one relationship between them. It is, however, Wittgenstein who frees himself from this entitative bias in the course of his book *Tractatus* itself. He shows that it is not the words but propositions which has meaning. Our sentences are no list of names or words, but a relationship of words which project a possible form. The realm of facts and the realm of language share a common logical structure. The propositions are meaningful when they picture the reality by projecting this common logical structure. But the problem continues to exist. If we accept Wittgenstein's proposal then meaningfulness can be ascribed only to the descriptive statements. Unfortunately, all our meaningful utterances are not descriptive in nature. There are many meaningful utterances which express command, instructions, emotions or simple rules of day-to-day conduct. If we stick to the Referential model then a large chunk of what we call meaningful propositions would be out of the bounds of meaningfulness.

Another radical form of Referential Theory surfaced during the 1930s. This theory was advocated by the Logical Positivists. They claim to be influenced by some of the remarks made by Wittgenstein in *Tractatus*. But it seems that they were more influenced by the methods of natural science. In their well-known 'verifiability criterion of meaning', they suggest that a statement in order to be meaningful must be verifiable, or else the statements must be concerning the rules of logic/mathematics or other *a-priori* sciences. Excluding these two forms of statements, other forms of statements are nonsensical in nature. I claimed that they were influenced by the methods of natural science, because it is believed that these two types of statements are used in science. But the Logical Positivists subsequently realised that all the statements of science are not verifiable in nature. Moreover, the laws of science are stated in the form of universal propositions. But universal statements are not verifiable. So the Logical Positivists, went on modifying their criterion and at last almost abandoned the criterion of verifiability. But it cannot be denied that the Positivistic theory of meaning is a form of Referential theory. And all forms of Referential theory narrows down the scope of meaning to the function of referring to the facts.

(ii) Ideational Theories : The Ideational theorists, on the other hand, believe that words do not stand for objective referents, but **ideas**. The ideas may be psychological or logical in nature. The British empiricist Locke advocated that meaning can be identified with psychical entities. For him, the primary unit of our language is a word, and the primary unit of our thought is an idea. the words must stand for ideas. As Locke says :

> The use, then, of words is to be a sensible mark of ideas; and the ideas they stand for are their proper and immediate signification.[23]

Hume is also a co-traveller of Locke, in this respect. He reduces thought in its ultimate analysis, to image. Words are associated with images; and this is the basis of determining the meaning. So the essence of meaning is identified with the accompanying mental states, that a word calls for. These ideas directly or indirectly refer to the sense-impressions or sense-datum that we get from the perceptual world. But this model fails as a theory of meaning. First of all, there are many words which are not accompanied by mental images. Moreover, ideas and images are private and particular. So they lack the desired universality, which must be shared by others to make the linguistic communication possible. Rather Plato's theory scores over this psychological account of meaning. Plato is bothered about the element of inter-personal nature of language. So he locates the objects of meaning in 'ideas'. Such ideas are not psychological states but universal class essence. I have discussed Plato's theory in my previous chapter. So without going into detail, we can say that such a logically promising theory somehow gets muddled by his acceptance of ontological status for the 'ideas'.

The logical explanation of meaning, in terms of ideas, comes from Bradley. He categorically states, "the idea **is** the meaning".[24] But such ideas are purely logical in nature. According to him ideas are pure, abstract and universal. The logical condition of our judgements reveal that everything has two aspects, the substantive part and the predicate part. Bradley calls the substantive part as **that** of a judgement which stands for the subject. The predicate part is called **what**, i.e., the content of a judgement. According to him, our judgement is an act by which we attach **what** (ideal content) to **that** (reality), which is beyond the act. So there is no brute fact to which we can jump with our judgements. The substantive part is purely logical in nature. It is neither meaningful nor meaningless. So meaning is adjectival in nature, it is the 'what' of the proposition, which adds meaningfulness to the subject part. But the predicate and adjectival content is a part of the 'meaning-whole' or the 'ideal-content'. The ideal-content is purely universal and abstract in nature, and 'wandering adjective'.[25] which we cut loose from conceptual net and apply it to contexts which mind has fixed. The ideal content or meaning is the one and the whole, a complex totality of qualities and relations. It is we, the language speakers, who introduce division and distinction, and call these products separate ideas with relation between them. So every judgement is a part of this whole, it is not just a relation between two particular ideas, i.e., subject and predicate.

Here, we note that Bradley's analysis is completely different from the other theories of meaning, we have discussed so far. Other theories, be it Referential or Ideational, analyse meaning in terms of words, not sentences. Moreover, such theories concentrate on particular statements and the conditions of their meaningfulness. Bradley's theory of meaning represents more or less, a metaphysics of meaning. And in certain respects it is very similar to that of Bhartṛhari's theory of *śabdādvaitavāda*. Like Bhartṛhari, he believes that the 'meaning-whole' or 'language-whole' cannot be expressed as such. What we present through our language are 'bits' or 'pieces' of the 'meaning-whole' by selecting and fixing a particular part of it. Our language does not refer to facts directly. The brute realm of facts are not graspable by the 'bits' of language. However, there is a big difference between Bradley's and Bhartṛhari's metaphysics. For Bhartṛhari, the Absolute metaphysical principle is of the nature of language, (*śabda*). But Bradley's Absolutism is not an Absolutism of language. Besides Bhartṛhari does not analyse language in terms of 'that' and 'what'. If there is such linguistic distinction between 'that' and 'what', Bhartṛhari would rather say that both belong to the 'ideal content' or the 'meaning-whole'.

(b) Non-Essentialism

Let us now revert back to our discussion on the theories of meaning. We have seen that the essentialistic approach is based on determining an essence for meaning. Wittgenstein, in his book *Philosophical Investigations*, took to task his own Essentialistic interpretation of meaning in *Tractatus,* his early work. In total opposition to what he said earlier in *Tractatus* he declares that meaning does not represent an essence. It is rather futile to fix a definition for meaning, because it is not the name of an entitative concept, but a function. It is the function of 'use'. So to understand the true nature of meaning, we must see it 'at work'. With this new way of handling the problem of meaning in his book *Philosophical Investigations* he brings to our notice three main aspects of philosophy of language: (i) Language is an **act**. It is the act of communication. So we must take into consideration the role of speaker, hearer and the context of speech, (ii) Meaning is a question of workability and applicability in diverse human situations; (iii) the true nature of language cannot be unravelled in terms of strict structural rules and ideal language. We have to keep ourselves at the level of ordinary language and watch its diverse forms of use.

We need not discuss all the aspects of Wittgenstein's philosophy of language. But it will suffice to say that Wittgenstein's later philosophy marked the beginning of a new way of doing philosophy. Wittgenstein in his *Tractatus* concentrates on the structural and semantical aspects of language. But now he shifts his attention to the functional and pragmatic aspect of language. His dictum 'Don't ask for the meaning, ask for use' — brings into prominence the communicative dimension of language. If we notice the phenomenon of language at work, we find that language has multiple facets. It can be used to mean varied sorts of activities. As Wittgenstein points out, we can use language to report facts, to play, to pray, to tell stories and to do many more things. So he discards his early view. He says that the relation between the word and meaning is not like:

> Here the word, there the meaning. The money and the cow you buy with it. (But contrast: money, and its use).
> (*P.I.* 120)

By highlighting the functional aspect of language he successfully shows that our language does have multiple functions and forms. Meaning can be determined in various ways depending on what activity is intended to be performed by its use and the context of its use. He compares language with a tool box. As the tool box contain varied sorts of tools, and each of them are meant for specific functions, similarly language performs varied sorts of function. The rule of one 'language-game' cannot be applied to another form of game. We cannot decide the meaningfulness of a factual statement with the criterion that is meant for understanding a moral statement. There are multiple forms of language, and multiple ways of deciphering their meanings. In short, for him 'diversity' is the key word not 'unity'.

This new way of approaching the problem of meaning brought

in its wake many new-theories, each highlighting one or the other aspect of communicative role of meaning and language. Most prominent amongst them are Grice's and Austin's theory. Grice in a small paper entitled 'Meaning', brought into focus the role of the speaker and the importance of 'intention' in the communication of meaning. Austin in his book *How to Do Things With Words* showed the different levels of **acts** in the performance of a communication. He very explicitly showed the distinction between the 'meaning' which is the propositional content of the utterance, and the 'force' which reflects the speaker's intention in uttering a statement. Searle developed Austin's theory of speech-acts to elicit the basic structural conditions involved in speaker's utterances as well as in hearer's understanding. Davidson, on the other hand, focused on the semantical aspect of communicative meaning by adopting a modified version of Tarski's semantical notion of truth. And we expect many more theories of language and meaning to emerge in future.

Another new trend in philosophy also emerged from Wittgenstein's emphasis on diversity and non-essentialism. Wittgenstein in *Philosophical Investigations* advocates that language is not only communicative but it represents the forms of life. Human life and experience is multi-dimensional, and accordingly language too has multiple facets. So the criterion of meaningfulness cannot be put into the straightjacket of an uniform definition. Each form of language has its own rules of acquiring meaningfulness. The logic of understanding one form of language cannot be applied to understanding the significance of another form of language. When I say 'This table is red' and 'X is good' — both are meaningful statements. But the former is a descriptive statement and the latter is an evaluative statement. I can discern the meaning of the former statement on the basis of its reporting a state of affairs. But in case of the latter statement no such facts are stated. I cannot verify the 'goodness' of a man in the sense I verify the 'redness' of a table. This sort of analysis gave rise to specialised branches of philosophy such as, philosophy of religion, philosophy of morality, etc. In such specialised studies philosophers take up for analysis the specific nature of language used in, say, statements of ethics, or religion, etc.; and the nature and meaning of such statements are delineated. Holistic understanding of language, as a result, is replaced by fragmentalised and piecemeal analysis.

Bhartṛhari on Different Layers of Meaning

Keeping in our mind these new trends of handling the issues of language and meaning, let us assess Bhartṛhari's position. To the question 'what does a word mean ?' — Bhartṛhari's answer would be, "that which is communicated by the speaker to the hearer". Here Bhartṛhari's way of looking at meaning cannot come within the fold of essentialistic theories of meaning. Nor is it non-essentialistic in Wittgensteinian sense. No doubt, he would admit that language is not necessarily descriptive. It is clear from the examples he uses in his treatise that he admits of varied forms of linguistic usage. Once he admits the communicative role of language, the varieties of meaning communicated are automatically taken for granted. But this does not result in fragmentalised view of communicated meaning. But how does the hearer discern different forms of meaning communicated ? Does he confuse the reporting of facts with the subtle emotions expressed in poetry ? In Bhartṛhari's scheme there is no scope for such confusion, nor is there any necessity for the hearer to have the knowledge of the structure of different forms of language. The task of discerning the meaning is left to the inherent linguistic intuition called *pratibhā*. So variety of forms of linguistic utterances do not figure very prominently in Bhartṛhari's philosophy. He treats language as a 'whole', which is expressible in multiple number of ways.

(a) Primary and Metaphorical Meaning

One of the most remarkable features of Indian way of looking at language is that all the systems of thought conceive language as communicative. The other important feature is understanding the concept of meaning from the hearer's stand point. Therefore, the problems they encounter is of a different nature. They undertake to examine the different shades of meaning which the hearer encounters, such as literal meaning, intended meaning, contextual meaning, metaphorical meaning, suggestive meaning, etc. They also undertake to examine certain common linguistic features such as the use of homonyms, synonyms and ambiguous words. And also they offer clues for discerning the meaning of ambiguous words.

It is a fact, that our ordinary language is very flexible and fluid. To bound it by the strict rules of one word-one meaning relation will stiffle its naturalness. We can do many things with words, we can turn and twist a word to mean different ideas. Therefore in all natural languages we come across the problem of varied shades of meaning. Bhartṛhari takes up the peculiarities of language-in-use with all sincerity and tries to solve the problems arising out of the peculiarities of linguistic usage. First we have the problem of metaphorical transfer of words. This is most often based on similarity or contiguity, and shifts in meaning. In such cases, a distinction must be made between the primary meaning and the secondary meaning, otherwise the force of the metaphor will be lost. But how do we make the distinction between the primary and metaphorical meaning ? In Indian Philosophical literature we come across varied interpretation of metaphorical meaning of words. In his *Vākyapadīya*, Part-II, Bhartṛhari discusses different popular views available on the topic.[26] But it should be kept in mind that for him the primary unit of meaning is a sentence, not a word. And he also believes that the meaning is not necessarily grasped from the knowledge of individual words used in a sentence. Still he does not mind discussing the question of the distinction between the primary and metaphorical meaning of words. Some of the popular views stated by him are as follows.

(i) According to those who hold that a word can have more than one meaning, the distinction between primary and secondary meaning is based on the relative frequency of the usage. The meaning with which a word is frequently and generally used is the primary meaning.

(ii) There are others, who hold that a word can have only one sense, who believe that the word having the primary sense and the words having secondary sense are actually different words, though they sound alike.

(iii) Another theory attributed to *Vyādi*, is that the primary meaning of a word is that which is well-known; and which only depends on its form. But the secondary meaning is established with effort, with the help of some context.

(iv) According to yet another view, words refer to the qualities. That object which possesses these qualities to a greater extent is called the primary meaning and the other is called the secondary meaning. Bhartṛhari does not support this view, because this is not the pattern followed in our actual usage.

(v) Another view regarding this distinction, is totally different. According to it, the metaphorical or secondary usage is based on similarity. "Devadatta is a lion" means that Devadatta possesses those qualities similar to that of a lion.

Though Bhartṛhari takes care to present these popular views, his stand regarding the issue is totally different. According to him the metaphorical meaning, or any other form of intended meaning can be deciphered only in the context of a sentence, and the particular situation in which the sentence is uttered. Thus when a mother says "the tiger eats children who cry" — any sensible hearer will understand that the intended sense is to induce some fear in the child so that he will stop crying. Again in cases like ironical statements, the meaning of the individual words taken together gives a different sense, than the sense intended in the context. Therefore Bhartṛhari argues that words as such cannot have metaphorical meaning. It is only the sentence and the context of utterance which can determine whether the sentence expresses the literal meaning or metaphorical meaning.

(b) Literal Sense and Contextual Meaning

As Bhartṛhari emphasises the role of sentence as the primary conveyor of meaning, he offers a detailed account of deciphering the intended meaning by the hearer. We have noted earlier that some Indian philosophers take *tātparya* as one of the conditions of sentence-meaning. *Tātparya*, literally means significance, but in the context of sentence it implies the significance derived from the contextual factors. In a linguistic communication the speaker expresses his intention (*abhiprāya*), but unless the hearer grasps the intended meaning, the communication fails. It is well-known that our natural language is full of ambiguous words. So the hearer has no way but to refer to contextual factors to understand the sense of an utterance. Bhartṛhari was one of the earliest philosophers to recognise this peculiarity of natural language. The speaker can use the words to express the literal sense and also to express some intended sense. Therefore Bhartṛhari gives an account of how meanings can be rendered precise with the help of contextual factors, as well as syntactical factors. Briefly they may be stated as follows :[27]

(i) Association — The word *Hari* may be used to mean various things. It is the name of God Viṣṇu, it may also mean a monkey. But the term *Hari* used in association with *Hari*, "with conch and discus", would make it clear, that by *Hari* lord Viṣṇu is meant.

(ii) Dissociation — The word *dhenu* may mean a cow or a mare. But the sentence "*dhenu* without calf" is unambiguous, because the phrase "without calf" implies a dissociation which makes it clear that we are talking of a cow which is now without the calf.

(iii) Mutual association — When somebody says '*Rāma* and *Lakṣmaṇa* went to forest', we decipher that '*Rāma*' means the brother of *Lakṣmaṇa*, not Balarāma (the brother of *Kṛṣṇa*) or *Paraśurāma*. Here the meaning of *Rāma* is recognised on the basis of mutual association of *Rāma* with *Lakṣmaṇa*.

(iv) Hostility or opposition — *Chāyā* means 'beauty' or 'shade'. But in the compound phrase *chāyā* and *āloka* (light) the meaning of *chāyā* obviously implies 'shade'. This is because of the opposition of meaning between the light and shade.

According to Matilal all these four factors can be called the general determination of meaning through association. It is mostly a case of psychological association.[28]

(v) Purpose — *Sthānu* means a pillar or Lord *Śiva*. In the sentence "worship *sthānu*" the purpose of the speaker is obviously served when the term is understood in the latter sense.

(vi) Context or Situation — "Bring me *saindhava*", at the time of eating should mean 'salt', and at the time of going out should mean a 'horse'. Here the contexts determine the intended meaning of *saindhava*.

(vii) Indicatory sign — Some sign may be present in a larger context. In the context of a passage containing a ritual, when it is stated "wet pebbles are placed on the altar", it means wetting the pebbles with clarified butter. The pebbles as such can be soaked in any liquid, but in the larger context of a ritual the sentence means soaking in clarified butter. We have to understand it as an indicatory sign.

(viii) Proximity with another word — This is also a case of association. But it is not a case of psychological association. In such cases, physical proximity or syntactical connection is meant. The sentence 'God, the destroyer of cities' refers to Lord *Śiva.* Here the proximity or association of 'God' restricts the meaning to *Śiva,* otherwise 'kings' can also be meant by 'destroyer of cities' (enemy-cities).

(ix) Capacity — In the sentence "The cuckoo is intoxicated by *madhu*", *madhu* should mean, here, the spring season, not honey. The former sense of *madhu* (spring) has the capacity to intoxicate (in poetic sense) a cuckoo.

(x) Propriety — In the sentence "May your beloved's *mukha* protect you", *mukha* means 'favour', not 'face', since the former meaning will be proper in this context.

(xi) Place — In the sentence "There stands the master", 'the master' should mean the king not the God. The meaning of 'the master' is determined by the use of 'here' (the place).

(xii) Time — The sentence "*citrabhānu* shines", should mean "the sun shines" if uttered during the day, and "the fire or light shines", if uttered during the night.

(xiii) Gender and (n) accent — In some cases grammatical devices can resolve ambiguity. The word *mitra* in masculine gender means the sun, but in neuter gender means a friend. In the compound word "*indra-śatru* ", when the first syllable is accented it means "one whose killer is Indra". When the last syllable is accented it means "the killer of Indra.

The above list is not exhaustive, nor is mutually exclusive. Moreover, the contextual factors are determined by keeping the peculiarities of Sanskrit language in mind. But it is obvious that Bhartṛhari takes into account the grammatical factors, syntactical factors, psychological factors, contextual factors (both verbal and non-verbal), for determination of the intended meaning. All languages shares some of these features. But psychological and contextual factors definitely play a crucial role in the identification of intended meaning. However, prior to offering this exhaustive list, Bhartṛhari gives a limited yet more broad-based list of contextual factors. He says that the meaning of an expression is not to be determined merely by its form but by contextual factors also. They are — syntactical relation, purpose, situation, propriety, place and time.[29] These factors are more universal in nature and not related to a specific language (in this case, Sanskrit). If we go by the spirit of what Bhartṛhari says about the problem of word-meaning relation and communicability of language, it becomes clear that he deals with the problems in a comprehensive manner.

Bhartṛhari and Wittgenstein on Diversities of Meaning

I will like to conclude this chapter with an interesting point that emerges from our discussion here. Both later Wittgenstein and Bhartṛhari start with the presumption that language is communicative, and language can be used to express varied sorts of meanings. Despite this, their analysis of language results in radically different conclusions. Bhartṛhari's analysis ends up with a holistic view of language, on the other hand Wittgenstein's analysis ends with a diversified account of language. This difference may be ascribed to their inherent purpose in taking up the problem of language. Bhartṛhari was a Grammarian-philosopher, so his avowed task was to examine everything in terms of 'what language presents'. Wittgenstein, on the other hand, was more or less perturbed by the confusions and muddleheadedness created by the philosophers being 'duped' by linguistic elements. In his *Philosophical Investigations* he investigates the nature of language to use it as a therapy. This is clear from the following passage:

> Of course what confuses us is the uniform appearance of words when we hear them spoken or meet in script or print. For their **application** is not presented to us so clearly. Especially not, when we are doing philosophy.
> (*P.I.*, Sect. II)

The language that we ordinarily speak, often leads us to form a picture of reality. And these pictures entrap us in some form of generalised world-view. Therefore, he conceives that the task of the philosopher is not to be trapped by the structural and grammatical analogies presented by language :

> Philosophy is a battle against the bewitchment of our intelligence by means of language.
>
> (*P.I.*, Sect. 109)
>
> Philosophy . . . . is a fight against the fascination which forms of expression exert upon us.
>
> (*Blue and Brown Book,* p. 27)

Wittgenstein perhaps would have said that the forms of language 'duped' Bhartṛhari too. The picture of 'word' as all-pervasive phenomenon held him captive. So the ultimate aim of Bhartṛhari and Wittgenstein, in handling the concept of language and meaning are radically opposite.

References

1. *Vāk.*, I.86.
   Also *Vṛtti* under I.170, II.19, II.31.
2. "Just as the mind of the speaker first turns towards the word, in the same way, the attention of the hearer is also first directed towards them. *Vāk.*, I.53.
   "The word is examined in the mind, is then fixed to a specific meaning, and then through the instrumentality of word-sounds is produced (through their causes)
3. *Vāk.*, I.57.
4. *Vāk.*, I.50.

   ātmarūpam yathājñāno jñeyarūpam ca dṛsyate |
   artharūpam tathā śabde svarūpam ca prakāśate ||

5. *Vāk.*, I. *See* Iyer's translation, p. 102.1.4.
6. *Vāk.*, II.32.
7. *Vāk.*, I.50.
8. *Vāk.*, I.56
9. *Vāk.*, III.3.1.2.
10. *Ibid.*
11. *Ibid.*
12. Iyer, *Bhartṛhari,* p. 204.
13. *Vāk.*, III.3.2.
14. Iyer, *Bhartṛhari,* p. 205.
15. *Vāk.* Quoted in *Śabda Śakti Parikṣā* :

ājānikas cādhunikaḥ saṅketo dvividho mataḥ nitya ājānikas tatra ya śaktir iti giyate, kadācitkas tvādhunikaḥ śāstrakārādibhiḥ kṛtaḥ

(Refer K.K. Raja, *Indian Theories*, p. 23)

16. Iyer, *Bhartṛhari*, pp. 207-8.
17. *Ibid.*, p. 206.
18. *Vāk.*, I.68-69.
19. Iyer, *Bhartṛhari*, p. 211.
    Vāk., III.3.61-71.

    Linguistic usage does not proceed with this transcending Reality as its basis. Its basis is rather what is **thought** to exist, what is conceptually constructed (As summarised in *Encyclopaedia of Indian Philosophies*, Vol. 5, p 159).
20. *Vāk.*, I.68-69.
21. *Vāk.*, III.1.6.

    svājātiḥ prathamam śabdaiḥ sarvair ebābhidhiyate, tato' rthajātirūpeṣū tadadhyāropa kalpanā |
22. *Vāk.*, III.3.1-2.

    sarva parsad punaridam śāstramiti ye vahysyārthasya śabdavacatvam nechanti tanmatopa saṅgrahārtha vākyābhiprāya rūdhasaiva śabdārthatve tatra kārya kāraṇa saṁbandhamaha |
23. John Locke, *Essay Concerning Human Understanding*, Book-III, Ch. 2, Section-I.
24. F.H. Bradley, *Principles of Logic-I*, London : Oxford University Press, 1922, p. 6.
25. *Ibid.*, p. 10.
26. *Vāk.*, II.265-67, 274, 275, 276, 280.
27. *Vāk.*, II.317 f.
28. Matilal, *Word and World*, p. 25.
29. *Vāk.*, II.316.

    vākyāt prakaraṇāt arthād aucityād deśakālataḥ, śabdarāthaḥ pravibhajyante na rūpād eva kevalāt |

5

Language and Communication

Formalism versus Communication-Intention Theory

BHARTṚHARI conceives language not as a string of dead and sterile syllables but as an act. Language gets its life by being used by the humanity in their exchange of thought and expression. In short, language is communicative in nature. In the context of modern philosophers' interest in communicative role of language, let us examine how they formulate and solve this problem of communication; and how Bhartṛhari looks at the issue.

The philosophical discussions on the problem of language and meaning during the last four decades are dominated by two distinctive strands of thought. On the one hand the Formalists like Frege, early Wittgenstein, Chomsky projected language as a rule-governed activity, on the other hand the Communication-intention theorists like later Wittgenstein, Grice, Austin and others highlighted the functionalistic and communicative dimension of language. Both the schools agreed that the language was a rule-governed activity but the point of their difference was regarding what should be the primary basis of meaning. For the Formalists **linguistic meaning** is primary, whereas for the latter, the **communicative meaning** is primary. In other words, the Communication theorists argue that the fundamental concept of meaning should be understood in terms of 'speaker's **meaning something by** an audience-directed utterance on a particular occasion'. As a result they contest the Formalists' thesis that the rules of syntax and convention are all, that is to be explicated if one has to understand the concept of language. They rather insist that the rules and conventions are explicable in terms of the communication-intention. Grice even goes to the extent of arguing that it is possible to expound the concept of communicative meaning without presupposing the notion of linguistic meaning. He shows that a system of convention can be modified to adjust to the needs of intention to communicate, which we can scarcely imagine to exist before the system existed. And these modifications in turn can create the possibility of thought which would not have been possible without presupposing these modifications. This proves that language is not just a reproductive activity on the part of the speaker, it is creative too. There is always a scope for modifications and enlargements in the area of linguistic meaning, which ultimately makes language a living affair. There is always an interplay between the rules and conventions on the one hand, and the intention to communicate on the other. As Strawson succinctly puts it, "Primitive communication-intentions and successes give rise to the emergence of a limited conventional meaning-system, which makes possible its own enrichment and development which in turn makes possible the enlargement of thought and communication needs to a point at which there is once more pressure on existing resources of language which is in turn responsive to such pressure. And of course there is an element of mystery in this; but so there is in human intellectual and social creativity any way".[1] The Communication-intention thesis definitely unfolds a very important dimension of language by exploring beyond the limits of the linguistic meaning. One may not agree with Grice on the point that communication-intention itself is sufficient to explain the conception of meaning without any reference to the rules of convention and syntax. But at the same time, nobody can deny that a close relation between the communicative needs and rules of convention should be presumed if one has to conceive language as a living social affair. Still it seems that the presumption about this relationship is not adequate enough if one intends to investigate the nature of language and its capacity to convey meaning. It becomes mandatory for him to examine the nature of the relationship between the communicative intention and the rules of syntax and convention. The element of creativity that is a part of linguistic expression which Strawson prefers to leave aside by calling it "an element of mystery", should be explored further to have a comprehensive idea about the true basis of the communicative role of language. Besides, there are certain baffling questions about linguistic communicability which needs considerable attention, viz., Is linguistic communication possible just because the speaker expresses his intention to communicate through the uttered speech ? If so, then why in certain cases, the hearer, in spite of listening to the complete utterance by the speaker, fails to grasp the meaning ? Again how in certain cases, even before the speaker has completed his utterance, the hearer grasps the meaning ? These questions make one uncomfortable about accepting the communication-intention theory of meaning without probing further into some of the basic concepts of communication. For any thinker who advocates the theory of communicative meaning, explication of three primary ideas becomes mandatory, viz., (i) the speaker, (ii) the hearer, and (iii) the common bridge of inter-subjectivity. The **speaker** is the one, who not only utters certain strings of words, but also **intends** to communicate his thought or belief to somebody. Moreover, he not only intends to communicate but through his speech-act, he intends 'to secure an uptake' (if I may be allowed to borrow the phrase from Austin) from the hearer. The **hearer** is the person who **understands** what the speaker intends to communicate through his utterance. He follows it up either by speaking his reactions, or by acting in accordance with the speaker's intention. But the most crucial concept in case of communicative interpretation of meaning is providing a ground for the inter-subjectivity. In other words, one has to explain how the meaning is transferred from the speaker to the hearer ? The obvious answer to such a question seems to be : because the speaker and the hearer belong to the same linguistic community, they share the same rules and conventions of the 'language-in-use'. This answer seems so obvious that it prompts David Lewis to remark, "It is a platitude — something only a philosopher would dream of denying — that there are conventions in language".[2] But the philosopher is like a devil, who often loves to tread the area where the angel dreads to step. And he does it with success and sufficient justifications. So philosophers of language analyse the concept of 'convention' and examine whether it can serve as a solid bridge for communication between the speaker and the hearer. Before I take up how the Communication-intention theorists handle the issues, I deem it fit to discuss Bhartṛhari's views on the notion of language, meaning and communicability.

Bhartrhari on Language

Bhartṛhari handles the problems of meaning and language in a more comprehensive manner without assuming any gulf between the two ways of looking at things. He shows that there is an interplay between the need for communication and the rules of syntax and convention. But obviously his theory seems to be more favourably inclined towards communication-intention theory of meaning. He would agree with these theorists in ascertaining that the intention to communicate is conceptually prior to the rules of convention. For convention itself cannot be the basis of language. The rules of convention presupposes the use of meaningful communication in some form or other.[3] Rather, according to Bhartṛhari the uttered level of speech, which requisitions use of rules, is not the whole language. It is like the tip of the ice-berg. Though the level of utterance is a very important phase of linguistic expressibility, it is not the whole of it. Even when the uttered speech is not at work, our linguistic competency does not slumber, for this is the very basis of our thought, consciousness, as well as knowledge of the world. Anything that exists is as good as non-existent unless and until it is named and linguistically conceived. So the phonetic level of speech is nothing but externalisation of the very speech-potentiality present within us. Our phonetic expressions are not simply sounds caused by air and the vocal organ. It is the manifestation of *śabda tattva* or linguistic potency or linguistic principle. This potency is manifested through *prāṇa* (breath) and *buddhi* (intellect).[4] So when a speaker intends to say something he thinks of the appropriate words to express his thought through verbal means. What remains at the level of thought finds expression in the form of utterances with the help of vocal organ and articulation.

We have noted in Chapter 3 that the essence of Bhartṛhari's theory of meaning is epitomised in the concept of *sphoṭa* (the linguistic potency). This potency is manifested through three phases: (i) *paśyantī*, the non-verbal level of unitary meaning-whole, (ii) *madhyamā*, the pre-verbal level of mental speech-activity, and (iii) *vaikhārī*, the verbal and phonetic level of speech.

(a) Structural and Functional Components of Utterance

Since the modern discussions on language centres on the concept of uttered speech, it will be preferable for us to start with

Bhartṛhari's analysis of *vaikhārī vāk*. This offers us a better scope to explicate his views in modern idiom; and also allows us to note how much of it is relevant and how much of it has become obsolete with time. The first and foremost point which I want to emphasize is that for Bhartṛhari, our uttered speech is not just a string of inert and sterile symbols, it is an **act** of doing certain things. This is clear from his concept of *artha pravṛtti*. He specifies : "On language depend the principles governing the practical purposive activities.... What depends on language may be the speaker's intended meaning, the possibility of applying a word to thing, the ability to combine words into sentences, the connecting of objects with actions, identification of a thing as to be accomplished or the projection of the content of an awareness as an external object".[5] With this, he brings into limelight the various types of activity involved in speaking and using the utterances. But very broadly speaking, language is used as a means of expressing the speaker's intention. This intended meaning may refer to facts both physical and mental or may be used to accomplish certain acts, i.e., the act of commanding, questioning, stating etc. This shows that the *vaikhārī vāk* is a very important phase of the analysis of *śabda*.

If we look at the constitutive factors of *vaikhārī vāk*, we will note that, for Bhartṛhari it is a complex network of many important elements. Initially Bhartṛhari identifies two. According to him, in any expressive language, two elements can be deciphered, i.e., the sound-pattern and forms of words (*dhvani*) and the meaning (*śabda*). But an elaborate study of his treatise shows that apart from these two, some other elements are also involved in the act of speech. Accordingly, I shall try to bring into notice four important constitutive elements of the uttered speech, they are: (a) sound-pattern (the phonetic element), (b) form of words (syntactic element), (c) meaning (semantic element), (d) intention of the speaker (pragmatic element).

He identifies the phonetic element as *dhvani* or *nāda*. The *dhvani* occurs due to the presence of our vocal organ. The phonetic element is characterised by variations in accent, pitch, intonations from speaker to speaker. Of course, later on, he introduces a subtle distinction between two levels of *dhvani*, i.e., *prākṛta dhvani* and *vaikṛta dhvani*. The former represents the sound-pattern vocally unmanifested and the latter represents vocally manifested sound.

So to be specific, we must say that, at the level of utterance the phonetic element can be identified as the *vaikṛta dhvani.* We shall discuss about *prākṛta dhvani* later on. The *vaikṛta dhvani* gives vent to the structure and forms of words. The second element, i.e., *vācaka* is the expressive linguistic form which is the conveyer of meaning. The role of the forms and structures of expressive words (*vācaka*) is very crucial, for it is **that** to which the hearer pays attention when the speaker wants to communicate through utterances. It is the element which has to be recognised by the hearer before he grasps the meaning of the utterance and the speaker has to think of it before he expresses his thought. Bhartṛhari points out, "Both the speaker and the hearer have to think of the word first before thinking of the meaning".[6] But people intent on understanding meaning, often fail to recognise the distinction between the expressive words and the expressed meaning. In fact, the *vācaka,* the forms and structures of words are just the bearer of meaning. It is the symbol which symbolises the meaning. This brings us to the third element of *vaikhāri vāk,* i.e., the *vācya* (the meaning/content). *Vācya* is that which finds expression through phonetic and syntactic element. So there is a close relationship between *vācya* and *vācaka* because the words have a natural fitness (*yogyatā*) to express meaning. It is a relationship of the conveyer and the conveyed, which is otherwise known as *vācya-vācaka bhāva.* However the element of meaning considered in isolation stands for certain unitariness which is diversified by sequential nature of the uttered words. The whole meaning cannot be expressed simultaneously, because our utterances by nature are sequential. We utter words syllable by syllable; and the moment one syllable is uttered it is replaced by another syllable. It should be noted here that not only Bhartṛhari, but most of the schools of Indian philosophy point to this peculiarity of the uttered speech. The philosophers of the present century have not paid much attention to this peculiarity. It seems that they consider it to be an insignificant characteristic. But in Indian philosophy of language, this characteristic of uttered speech occupies an important place. They consider that the question of communicability of meaning cannot be settled unless and until one decides how the discreet and sequential phonemes and syllables convey the unitary meaning to the hearer. This issue gets much attention in Indian philosophy of language, because they explicate meaning not only from the speaker's standpoint, but hearer's too. The hearer has to attend to the sequential speech form to get the sequenceless meaning out of it. So the element of meaning is in a sense unitary, expressed in a diversified form through the uttered words. The fourth element of the uttered level of speech is the intention of the speaker. "The uttered level of speech is possible, because the speaker intends to communicate".[7] The relationship between the speech and intention is named as *kārya-kāraṇa bhāva*. Bhartṛhari points out that it is the intention of the speaker which necessitates the use of particular forms of words. So it is a relationship of *kārya* (cause). "When the speaker seeks to superimpose linguistic forms onto his intended meaning, the language appears to change its nature into something else (meaning) and project it as sounds from the vocal organ".[8]

Apart from these four elements, the uttered speech, the *vaikhārī vāk* necessarily implies the issue of referring. The act of referring is no part of the phonetics and syntax, it is rather the function of the meaning. What is meant or conveyed has the function of referring. When one utteres the word *ghaṭa* (jar) it refers to the objectt *ghaṭa*. There need not be a one-to-one relationship between the meaning and object, nor does the act of reference imply the existence of the object. We may as well refer to the entities that do not exist at all, such as the 'wheel of fire', or 'hare's horn'. The act of meaning is not confined to stating facts only. It can be used in various ways such as eliciting acts as in the case of the command 'bring water'; or refer to certain mental states, or even to understand the forms of language. The act of meaning has the primary function of making all sorts of cognition possible. Therefore, the understanding of *vaikhārī vāk* remains incomplete if we analyse it only from the standpoint of the **speaker**. **Hearer** is an important factor too. So in Indian philosophy of language, the concept of *śabdabodha* or the hearer's understanding is given a very important place. The functionalistic interpretation of language makes it imperative to examine the concept of hearer's understanding. Bhartṛhari remarks, "Hearer's knowledge of a sentence arises from the words of the speaker and it reaches him through the words, and these words having been understood ends in the shape of knowledge, which is again in the form of words".[9] Further elaborating this concept of hearer's meaning, B.K. Matilal says, "The structured thought that is supposed to arise in such an ideal hearer is something that is inter-subjectively available: it is presumably shared by any competent language user who hears the sentence uttered".[10]

At present it will suffice for us to note the two most important consequences that follow from the inclusion of hearer's role in the analysis of uttered speech. First, Bhartṛhari strongly advocates that **sentences**, not the **words** are the primary units of the meaning communicated. Second, a distinction is to be maintained between the linguistic meaning and the intended meaning. Regarding the former issue, a series of arguments and counter arguments are recorded in the history of Indian philosophy. Bhartṛhari offers some very subtle yet incisive arguments in favour of the sentence-meaning to silence his opponents who argue in favour of the primacy of word-meaning. But once a thinker admits the communicative theory of meaning and thereby admits the role of hearer, he cannot but accept that it is the sentence which conveys meaning. Even if the speaker utters just a word, the hearer understands it in sentential form. For example, when somebody comes running and utters 'fire', the hearer understands that 'some building or some object is on fire'. The primacy of sentence-meaning has been so unanimously accepted by present-day linguists and philosophers of language that it seems unnecessary to dwell on this point any further. So let us proceed to discuss the second point, i.e., the distinction between the linguistic meaning and intended meaning. Bhartṛhari does not elaborately discuss the issue. But he makes the point clear with several examples. While discussing the role of homophones, he indicates that in such cases the hearer must take into account the factors like situational-context and sentence-context to discern the intended meaning. Besides, in our day-to-day life, we come across the use of many sentences where the implied meaning is more important than the linguistic meaning. Bhartṛhari offers us some illuminating examples to prove this. When a traveller says to his companion, "We must go and look at the sun", the meaning conveyed by the speaker is not that of looking at the sun, but the hearer must realise how late it is in the day.[11] Similarly, in response to the command, "see that the crows do not steal the butter", not even the child is so literal minded to allow the dogs to steal the butter.[12] These examples in a way prove that the hearer has to grasp the intended meaning, not the linguistic meaning. The importance of the concept of intended meaning cannot be properly explicated if in the analysis of communicative meaning, the entire emphasis is shifted to speaker only.

(b) Language Beyond Utterance

Thus, so far we have been discussing the structural and functional components of the uttered speech, as envisaged by Bhartṛhari. It gives us sufficient scope to realise that Bhartṛhari succeeds, to a large extent, in focusing attention on the multiple facets of speech at the level of utterance. But Bhartṛhari does not believe that *vaikhārī vāk* or the uttered level is enough to explain the concept of linguistic communicability. Communication implies that speaker must say something and the hearer must understand him. But how the meaning is transferred from the speaker to the hearer ? Is meaning conceptually inseparable from words ? If this is so, then the same meaning could not have been expressed in different forms of sentences. If this is so, then one language could not have been translated into another language. Again, how in certain cases, does the hearer understand what the speaker intends, even if he mumbles something ? So it will be too simplistic to say that the meaning is conveyed because the speaker utters a string of sounds in accordance with the rules of grammar and syntax; and because the hearer follows the same rules, he will understand the meaning just by listening to the utterances.

Bhartṛhari's answer to such questions would be that utterances are just a part of the linguistic expressibility. The level of utterance points to the level of thought. Before the speaker uses the spoken words, he thinks of the appropriate words to express it. The hearer too, hears the sounds in a sequence and then thinks of the meaning that might be conveyed to him. This stage is known as the *madhyamā vāk*, the middle stage of linguistic expressibility. At this stage the distinction between the form of the words and the meaning is maintained. The sequentiality associated with spoken words is also present in *madhyamā vāk*. But the audibility of *vaikhārī vāk* is absent in *madhyamā* level. So interpreters identify it with the *prākṛta dhvani*, noted earlier. But this is not the ultimate ground of inter-subjectivity as well as linguistic expressibility. *Madhyamā vāk* refers to a still deeper level of thought known as *paśyantī vāk*. To understand the importance of this stage, we need to have a brief discussion on Bhartṛhari's conception of thought, cognition and awareness.

Bhartṛhari offers us a sort of linguistic cognitivism which is evident from the following remark : "There is no awareness of this world without its being intertwined with the word. All cognitive comprehensions appear to be penetrated as it were, with the word".[13] This remark should not be understood in the sense that all our thought and cognitions are nothing but as Plato would call it "the silent dialogue of soul". Nor does he advocate a sort of Pan-Psychologism. He simply puts forth that as Davidson would put it: "the two [language and thought] are indeed linked in the sense that each requires the other in order to be understood".[14] For Bhartṛhari the linkage between thought or cognitions or awareness and language is fundamental and essential. There can be no concepts without words and no words without concepts. Our consciousness itself is intertwined with the power of linguistic expressibility. Even our pre-linguistic awareness is not free from linguistic latency. If anything is cognitive, then it has a speech potential. This latent form of speech (*śabda bhāvanā*) is inherent in all conscious beings. So he says, "when everything is merged in the speech latency, no verbal usage can be accomplished in concept free awareness . . . Just as illumination is the nature of fire, just as consciousness is the nature of mind, likewise speech-latency is the nature of each awareness".[15] Of course, one should be cautious enough not to confuse speech-latency with the audible noise. "This does not mean that we always make audible noise with our vocal chord whenever we cognize, think or perceive anything. Nor is it proper to say that we make 'inaudible' noise. On the other hand, it implies that we verbalize at some **deeper** level as we cognize, and we cognize as we verbalize".[16] But, by tying up the notion of verbalisation with the concept of thought, is not Bhartṛhari taking recourse to a form of Psychologism ? Frege and early Wittgenstein avoided this path of analysing language and meaning on the ground that 'thought' implies a type of privatisation. We know that mental events and cognitive episodes are private, whereas language is public. The speech-latency, the latent form of speech, is something personal and private for each person. So this sort of explanation of meaning and language demolishes the 'objectivity' of language. But what Bhartṛhari argues is that *śabda-bhāvanā* (linguistic-latency) is expressible in audible speech and can break through the enclosure of privacy. It now becomes something which is inter-subjectively available. Besides, the consciousness intertwined with *śabda-bhāvanā* is something quite unlike "pain" that is purely private. Nobody can feel other's pain. It is something 'incurably private'. In this connection, we may take help from Bernard Williams' contrast between different paradigms of privacy. In case of 'pain', there is a difference between having the sensation of pain of oneself and thinking about someone else's having pain. The other is the case of episodic 'verbalisable' thought. The second case is 'curably private'. As Williams remarks, 'episodic thought which is totally verbal is nevertheless the nearest thing in the inner life to public thought".[17] In the true sense of the term, Bhartṛhari is not analysing the process of thinking, but the structural conditions of thought. I have resorted to this little digression to make the relation between thought and language clear, because Bhartṛhari's concept of *śabda bhāvanā* and his transference of the problem of language-analysis from the level of speech to thought may be misconstrued as a form of psychological explanation of meaning.

(c) Intention and Convention

So now we are in a position to come back to the original question, i.e., how is the interplay between the intention to communicate and conventional framework possible ? We have stated how the intention to communicate puts pressure on the existing convention-structure, and how this structure again leads us to think of newer ways to express ourselves. The principle of linguistic potentiality constantly forces us to enlarge the narrow confines of conventional forms. This makes language an act of creativity. Therefore, Bhartṛhari claims that the relationship between the forms of words and language is not conventional but eternal. There is a relationship of natural fitness (*yogyatā*) between the symbol and the symbolised, *vācya* and *vācaka*. This view may seem very inconsistent with what so far we have been discussing about Bhartṛhari's conception of linguistic communicability. If we accept this position at face value, then we have to admit that in Bhartṛhari's philosophy, there is no scope for enlargement and enrichment of vocabulary. To understand the true implication of Bhartṛhari's view, one must make a distinction between language as a principle and language as a form of usage. So let us look at Bhartṛhari's remarks on the issue. He says, "The natural fitness of a word to convey meaning is known to us through convention (*samaya* or *saṁketa*) which is understood as the observation of use of words by elders. This use follows the natural capacity of words to convey meaning and he does not create it. Human beings cannot create the relation between words and meaning whether we look upon the latter as eternal or transitory".[18] He again remarks : "Language is of two kinds, eternal and produced. The produced sort is involved in usage and reflects the nature of language. The eternal sort of language is the source of all usage, unsequenced, within everyone, the seat of all modifications, the locus of all actions, the basis of satisfaction and frustration . . ."[19] These statements make it clear that he considers language at two stages. The linguistic potency which manifests in the conveyance of meaning implies the power of words to express meaning. This power is not human creation. But at the empirical level, when language is taken as a type of expression (Hindi, English, etc.), then the relation between word and meaning is conventional. That the particularised form of language is conventional, is supported by Bhartṛhari's statement, "The grammatical treatises are composed from time-to-time by spiritual elite in deference to differing capacities of individuals by taking in consideration the changed capacities of expression as far as merit and demerit are concerned".[20] This amply proves that Bhartṛhari conceives the linguistic expressibility, the intention to communicate as conceptually prior to the conventions. This also explains how the interaction between the intention to communicate and enlargement of conventions and rules of language in use are possible. He does it through the concepts of speech-principle.

Language as a Function: Wittgenstein, Grice, Austin and Searle

So far we have been examining the basic presuppositions of Bhartṛhari regarding the question of linguistic communicability. Let us now take a brief stock of the recent developments in this field, keeping Bhartṛhari's account in the background. I admit, my analysis will be brief and sketchy. There have been such an upsurge of views and theories highlighting different dimensions of language in the present century that it is almost impossible to accommodate them within the narrow confines of the book. Since our task, at present, is confined to an assessment of communication-intention theory I shall concentrate on three philosophers, Grice, Austin and Searle; and discuss those aspects of their philosophy which are relevant for the purpose.

The awareness that language is not exclusively a matter of 'structure', but 'function' too, was crystallized after Wittgenstein advanced the dictum "Don't look for the meaning ask, for the use".

However, it was Grice who came out openly with a communicative interpretation of meaning in his paper entitled 'Meaning'. He emphasized two important dimensions of communicative role of language. First, meaning something by an utterance is as good as somebody intending to produce some effect on the hearer. As Grice specifies : "A meant something by X is (roughly), equivalent to A intended to produce some effect in an audience by means of recognition of his intention".[21] Secondly, there cannot be a simple meaningful linguistic expression without somebody (speaker) claiming to utter it. This sort of analysis makes it clear that Grice wants to obliterate the distinction between the 'linguistic' meaning and 'intended meaning'. In case of meaningful utterance what matters are the 'speaker' and his 'intention' to communicate. The hearer's role is not at all emphasized by Grice.

Austin, on the other hand, exposes some more complexities involved in case of linguistic expressibility. In his book *How to Do Things With Words*, he shows that saying something is **doing** something; **in** saying something we do something, and **by** saying something we do something. In short, language is a matter of **act** and it involves complex layers of acts. The most important feature of his analysis of language is that he gives us a comprehensive account of language in terms of phonetics, syntax, semantics and pragmatics. Moreover, by showing the distinction between 'meaning' and 'force' of an utterance he makes the elements of propositional meaning (sense and reference) and intended meaning a part of what is conveyed to the hearer. But still one may note that the hearer's role is neglected here. Of course, he talks of perlocutionary act as a separate category of act. Perlocutionary act refers to "the achievements of certain effects by saying something". But communication does not, in all cases, mean achieving certain effects on the thought, belief or action of the hearer. The hearer has to **understand** what the speaker means by his utterance. Therefore, perlocutionary act is an element of the speaker's meaning not hearer's meaning. As Searle very rightly points out "Human Communication has some extraordinary properties, not shared by most other kinds of human behaviour. One of the most extraordinary is this: If I am trying to tell someone something, then (assuming certain conditions are satisfied) as soon as he recognizes that I am trying telling him something and exactly what it is I am trying to tell him, I have succeeded in telling it to him".[22]

We find a proper balance between the convention and intention, and a balance between the speaker's meaning and hearer's meaning in the theory of Searle as propounded in his book *Speech Acts.* He agrees with Grice so far as he projects meaning as a communicative affair. But Searle does not go to the extent Grice goes in claiming that communication of meaning is exclusively a matter of intention, and not a matter of rules. Besides, Searle does not share Grice's view that meaning can only be defined in terms of intended effect on the hearer, because speaker does not always intend to produce such an effect on the hearer. On the other hand he agrees with Austin that "all linguistic communication involves linguistic acts", but he differs from Austin by analysing meaning not exclusively in terms of speaker's meaning but hearer's **understanding** of what is being conveyed.

Searle starts his investigation about the nature of language with three basic presuppositions:

1. Speaking a language is engaging in a rule governed activity.
2. Whatever can be meant can be said. (A given language may not have adequate vocabulary to say what we mean, but in principle, we can always express what we mean). This is otherwise known as the **Principle of expressibility.**
3. Sentence, not the word, is the unit of linguistic communicability.

Keeping these three presuppositions in mind let us understand how he explains the speaker's role, hearer's role, the concept of inter-subjectivity and the relation between convention and intention.

Speaking from the speaker's standpoint Searle identifies three levels of acts, i.e., (1) the act of uttering (utterance act), (2) the act of referring and predicating (propositional act), and (3) the act of expressing the intention (illocutionary act). Speaking from the hearer's stand the act involved is the act of **understanding**. While analysing the problem of linguistic communicability from the speaker's stand point, Searle makes a clear-cut dichotomy between the propositional act and illocutionary act, i.e., what the utterance **means** and what is **meant** by the utterance. Though he admits that in actual speech situation these elements are not separable, yet at the level of abstraction the distinction is of considerable importance. This distinction should not be understood simply in terms of linguistic meaning and intended meaning. It is something deeper than that. In each case of utterance there is the propositional element (the element of reference and predication) which is stated by the act of utterance. This is one of the reasons because of which the same propositional element can be used to indicate different intentions of the speaker, such as stating, warning, commanding, etc. But very broadly speaking, both the elements, i.e., the propositional element and force element, constitute the meaning that is conveyed by the speaker to the hearer. The hearer's understanding also includes the understanding of these two elements.

Now the crucial question for us is to understand what according to Searle is the common ground of inter-subjectivity between the speaker and the hearer. How does the hearer understand what the speaker wants to convey? Searle's answer is "the bridge between the speaker's side and hearer's side is provided by their common language".[23] This answer is apt to dissatisfy us. Is 'common language' enough to explain the concept of communicability ? Then why in certain cases the communication fails though speaker and the hearer share a common language ? Can't the person of a different linguistic community understand the speaker though the speaker uses a different language ? To elicit Searle's reply to such questions one must examine what Searle means by the term 'language' ? We know that he defines language as a 'rule governed activity'. But what are those 'rules'? Are they the rules of syntax and grammar set by the conventions adopted by a particular linguistic community ? Are they the rules of **language** or **particular languages** ? If he is talking about the rules of particular **languages** then he fails to achieve his avowed task of providing us with "philosophically illuminating description of certain general features of language".[24] Searle, of course, clarifies what he means by the rules of language, with the introduction of a distinction between the constitutive rule and regulative rule. According to him "regulative rules regulate antecedently or independently existing forms of behaviour . . . But constitutive rules do not merely regulate, they create or define new forms of behaviour".[25] He further argues that on the basis of our knowledge of constitutive rules of language one can translate sentences from one language to another. So he clearly states that : "When I say speaking a language is engaging in a rule governed form of behaviour, I am not concerned with particular conventions one invokes in speaking this language or that. . .but understanding the rules which conventions manifest or realise".[26]

So we can safely conclude that for Searle the basis of transferability of meaning from the speaker to the hearer is the common constitutive rules of language. When he says that language is not a matter of intention but convention too, he does not use the term 'convention' as it is ordinarily understood. By highlighting the concept of 'rules' he parts company with Grice, for he insists that not only phonetics and syntax is a matter of rule but the illocutionary act too is guided by rules. Of course, from such an explanation one must not conclude that Searle starts with Communication intention theory but ultimately comes back to a Formalistic interpretation of meaning and language. He strongly believes that meaning is communicative and the speaker's intention plays a major role in his analysis of speech acts. His presupposition that whatever is expressible can be stated meaningfully is a pointer to the fact that the existing rules of convention and syntax can be responsive to the needs of intention to communicate. Unlike Formalists, he believes that understanding the concept of language is incomplete without explicating the concept from the standpoint of communicability. So the conception of language as a rule governed behaviour along with the principle of expressibility leads him to analyse language in terms of speech acts, speaker's intention, hearer's understanding, propositional meaning and the rules governing the language. This makes his Communicative-intention theory of meaning more comprehensive. Yet certain questions remain unanswered. Even if the speaker and the hearer share the same constitutive rule, how come, in certain cases communication fails ? Again, how in certain cases the hearer understands what the speaker intends to convey without a complete utterance act and propositional act ? Such questions seem unanswerable as long as the analysis of meaning is confined to the level of speech acts.

Bhartṛhari and Searle on Linguistic Communication

However, one may note certain points of similarity between Bhartṛhari's and Searle's views on language. Searle's principle of expressibility, though not as sweeping as Bhartṛhari's notion of speech-latency (*śabda bhāvanā*), seems to hint at certain *a-priori* conditions of linguistic communicability. Both share similar views on the notion of conventional and pre-conventional notions of linguistic expressibility. Both accept that the sentence, not the word, is the unit of communicability. But one should not go on adding the points of similarity without carefully noting the basic differences in the approach of these two philosophers belonging to two different ages and two philosophical traditions.

For Bhartṛhari, linguistic communicability is a multi-layered affair, and without excavating the hidden layers beyond the uttered speech no analysis of language is complete. Therefore, he explicates the level of utterance with reference to the logical conditions of thought and cognition. But Searle avoids transgression into the area of 'thought'. He prefers to confine his analysis within the level of utterance and speech. He explains both, the speaker's **intention** and the hearer's **understanding** in terms of the constitutive rules of language. Though the analysis of meaning in terms of intentionality and mental episodes is no more considered to be a form of psychologism, yet in his book **Speech-Acts** he avoids the route.

The second and the most important divergence of approach emerges from the distinction maintained between the propositional element and force element. This distinction was originally conceived by Austin, and it has been welcomed by most of the subsequent philosophers. Though the concept of 'Proposition' is the cause of serious bafflement for the Western thinkers, yet it continues to dominate the area of philosophy of language. For Bhartṛhari, propositional element and force element have no distinctive purpose, because whenever a statement is uttered its meaning exhausts the force, excepting certain ambiguous expressions. In such cases contextual factors help the hearer to decipher the meaning. This difference of approach owes its origin to the role of 'proposition' in the Western philosophy of language. In this regard, B.K. Matilal's remark is very illuminating. He observes, "Indian philosophers and logicians do not operate with the notion of proposition, which is so well entrenched in the Western tradition. Let me explain : each cognitive episode, unique as it may be as an event, has a **structure** which gets expressed in a linguistic utterance, and by virtue of that **structure** it differs from another cognitive event. But the structure may coincide in totality with that of any other cognitive event, or events, taking place in the same person or different persons at the same time or at different times, in which case all these cognitive events will be structurally indistinguishable except by virtue of their temporality or by their occurrence in a different person or by both. All structurally indistinguishable cognitive events are treated by Indian philosphers insofar as their logical properties as well as philosophical analyses are concerned . . . The cognitive events, even when they are viewed and identified in this way, do not become propositions. The structural content is the minimal abstraction that is proposed here. The practice of the Indian philosophers, is to refer to cognitive events (structurally abstracted, but still treated as particular events) by identical linguistic expressions in which they are verbalised."[27]

It is, perhaps, because of such understanding of linguistic expressions, Indian Philosophers often refer to the mental level either in the form of *saṁskāras* or continuity in memory (as accepted by *Mīmāṁsā*) or in the form of *śabda bhāvanā* (as accepted by Bhartṛhari) to explain how the complete sense of meaning is grasped from the sequentially uttered speech. But such differences of standpoints are bound to exist when the analysis of problems are based on certain key concepts, which to a large extent, are determined by the period of time and cultural conditions. However, this should not deter us from understanding the ancient thought in terms of the present and enrichment of the present thought in terms of the wisdom of the ancients.

References

1. Strawson, P.F., "Meaning and Truth", In *Logico-Linguistic Papers*, London, Methuen and Co., 1974, p. 175.
2. Lewis, David, "Languages and Language", In *Language Mind and Knowledge*, ed. by Keith Gunderson, University of Minnesota Press, Minneapolis, 1975, p. 7.
3. This interpretation is offered by T.R.V. Murty in "Some Comments on the Philosophy of Language in the Indian Context", *Journal of Indian Philosophy*, 2. 1974, p. 326.
4. *Vāk.*, I. p.179, 1.2.f in K.A.S. Iyer's translation of *Vākyapadīya*, I. Bhandarkar Oriental Research Institute.
5. *Vāk.*, I.13.
6. *Vāk.*, I.53.
7. Helārāja on *Vāk.*, III, *Sambandha Samuddeśa*, 1.
8. *Vṛtti* on *Vāk.*, I.47-48. as summarized by Akjulkar and Potter.
9. *Vāk.*, I.50.
10. Matilal, B.K., *Language, Logic and Reality*, Delhi, Motilal Banarsidass, 1985, p. 417.

11. *Vāk.*, II.312.
12. *Vāk.*, II.314.
13. *Vāk.*, I.123.
14. B.K. Matilal, *Perception.*
15. *Vāk.*, I. *Vṛtti* under verses 123-24.
16. B.K. Matilal, *Perception*, p. 118.
17. *Ibid.*, p. 119.
18. *Vāk.*, III. Pt. I. p. 149. I. 9-10. K.A.S. Iyer's Translation.
19. *Vṛtti* on *Vāk.,* I.123-28. Akjulkar and Potter.
20. *Ibid.*, 135-37.
21. Grice, H.P., "Meaning", In *Philosophical Review*, July, 1957.
22. Searle, J.R., *Speech Acts : An Essay in Philosophy of Language*, London : Cambridge University Press, 1969, p. 47.
23. *Ibid.*, p. 48.
24. *Ibid.*, p. 4.
25. *Ibid.*, p. 33.
26. *Ibid.*, p. 41.
27. Matilal, B.K., *Perception*, p. 118.

6

Thought and Language

Nature of the Problem

TWENTIETH century philosphical preoccupation with language has mostly been confined to study of language in its relation to referents. However, no analysis of meaning can be complete if it does not take into consideration "what is the relation subsisting between 'thought', 'words' or 'sentence', and that which they refer to or mean".[1] Since the beginning of human civilization, when the man had already acquired the skill of communicating with language, he has been puzzled by the close relation between 'thought' and 'speech'. Even with the advancement of knowledge, when man started taking interest in syntax, grammar, semantics, and pragmatics of language, the basic connection between thought and language continued to perplex the philosophers. In this chapter we shall concentrate on this important issue. We shall mostly focus on the twentieth century philosopher's conception of the problem and his ways of handling it; and keeping this as the background we shall assess where Bhartṛhari stand. In other words, can we discard Bhartṛhari's view as primitive and obsolete, or does it transcend the onslaught of time ?

The relation between thought and language is a unique phenomenon of human life. It is usually believed that language serves for the expression of our thought. But it is not a one-way relationship, i.e., from the thought to language. It is a two-dimensional relation, as Strawson puts it ". . . it is surely right to say that. . . speech and writing express thought; that sentences are significant only insofar as they have power to do this. But if language in this way depends on thought, we must surely also feel for the force of the idea that we do not have just a one-way dependance; that, at a level of complexity, the availability in our language of a sentence for expressing a thought, in general, a condition of our possibility of thinking the thought."[2] However in the philosophical circles this two-way relationship between thought and language is discussed from two perspectives, first the perspective of philosophy of mind and secondly, the perspective of philosophy of language. I shall present these two ways of looking at things in brief. The basic problem for philosophers of mind is to examine how some basic elements associated with the concept of mind, such as 'concept', 'idea', 'thought' are language-dependent. In other words, they examine whether these concepts can be explained independent of linguistic elements or not. The philosophy of language looks at the problem the other way around. Their problem is whether the nature of language and its pattern of working, in any way, is connected with such mental phenomena, as 'thought', 'understanding', 'belief', 'concept', etc.

Bhartṛhari on Thought and Language

Now keeping this at the background let us see how Bhartṛhari analyses language-thought relationship.

To explicate Bhartṛhari's views on the topic, we must go back, again, to two very crucial passages of *Vākyapadīya* :

> *no so'sti pratyātayo loke yah śabdānumād ṛte* ।
> *anuviddham iva jñānam sarvaṁ śabdena bhāsate.* ॥
> (Vāk., I.123)

and,

> *vāgrupatā ced utkrāmed avavodhasya śāśvatī* ।
> *na prakāśam prakāśeta sā hi pratyavamarśinī* ॥
> (*Vak.*, 124)

They can be translated as follows:

> There is no awareness in this world without being intertwined with language. All congitive awareness appears as if it is interpenetrated with language.

> If the language-impregnated nature of awareness went away from it, then a cognition would not manifest (any object) of that (language impregnated nature) is the distinguishing nature of our cognitive awareness.
>
> (Translations adopted from B.K. Matilal's *The Word and the World*, p. 128.)

In the latter verse the use of the terms *prakāśa* and *pratyavamarśa* needs a further elucidation. Bhartṛhari, himself does not elucidate these two concepts in his *Vṛtti*. So we have to take help from the latter Grammarians: Utpala's and Abhinavagupta's interpretation of these terms. Utpala says that the very nature of illumination or *prakāśa* is *vimarśa*, i.e., discrimination, for otherwise cognitive illumination would be inert and passive like a material object such as a mirror or a crystal. Therefore, Bhartṛhari and other Grammarians believe that even in case of bare-awareness, our awareness is interpenetrated with *śabda* or *vāgrūpatā* (word-impregnation). Without such *vāgrūpatā* which Bhartṛhari identifies with *pratyavamarśa,* i.e., 'determination by word' (the latter Grammarians call it *vimarśa* or some time *parāmarśa*), an awareness is no awareness.

This theory claims that any sort of cognition and awareness has these two elements of 'illumination' and 'determination by word'. Matilal has explained the role of these two phenomena in the following way:

> Now 'illumination' means removal of darkness but simple removal of darkness does not reveal the object unless one is able to distinguish the outline of the object from its immediate surroundings or environment. Throwing a flood of light upon a canvas is only half of the process of showing the object; the picture of the object must be sufficiently distinguished from the background to make it visible. If *prakāśa* is the flood of light, *vimarśa* is what makes the object distinguishable and distinct. An awareness is thus both *prakāśa* and *vimarśa*, or to use modern Wittgensteinian jargon, an awareness is both showing and saying. The so-called pre-linguistic grasp of the object cannot be firm unless the object is sufficiently distinguished, and if it is sufficiently distinguished, *vimarśa* has already set in, and a *śabda bhāvanā* (penetration by word) is

> implicit. A pure *prakāsa* (illumination) without *vimarśa* (discrimination) is impossible in theory. In fact, it is not even like what such Western philosophers as Immanuel Kant or Nelson Goodman say, that perception without conception is mute and conception without perception is blind. It is rather like saying that perception without conception is blind and conception without perception is mute.[3]

Bhartṛhari's way of handling the concepts like 'cognition', 'awareness' and also 'concepts' may seem to be radical. But under no circumstances can it be called an analysis of psychological process. For him to be conscious being is almost identical with language-potent being. He says, "there is no being endowed with consciousness whose awareness of himself or others is not intertwined with word".[4] In fact this word-potency is the very basis of the distinction between the sentient (*sasaṁjña*) and which is insentient (*visaṁjñā*). "Any being which does not have this power (word-potency), cannot engage in purposeful activity. It is an insentient thing".[5] So the idea of something to be done in this world, depends upon language. Even the child when he shows the signs of activity has such understanding as is language-dependent. In a sense he implicitly argues that all our activities are prompted by some specific awareness of some purpose. And all such awareness, in turn, are linguistically impregnated.

From Bhartṛhari's argument it is, then, obvious that for him 'thought' in all its manifestations (be it cognition, perception, knowledge or even bare awareness), is inextricably related with language. However, from such a presentation of language-thought relationship it does not follow that for him 'thought' is nothing but "speech-disposition",[6] as it has been put forward by Wilfrid Sellars. We usually observe that language is the only way of knowing about what is going on inside our mind. This common way of looking at things has led us to believe that, of the language and thought, language is easier to understand and may be used to explain our thought. As Davidson has put this platitude:

> A primitive behaviourism, baffled by the privacy of unspoken thoughts, may take comfort in the view that thinking is really 'talking to one-self' — silent speech.[7]

Bhartṛhari would outright reject such a view. The verses of Bhartṛhari quoted earlier shows that the linkage is fundamental for him. As we have noted earlier, the central concept of Bhartṛhari's philosophy of language is *sphoṭa*. This has two elements, the element of being expressible in the form of uttered words and the element of its meaning or the thought that the uttered words convey. They are inseparable and are rather like the two sides of the same coin. "Hence the words and concepts they convey cannot very well be separated in this view".[8]

> *Śabdanā*, 'languageing', is thinking; and thought 'vibrates' through language. In this way of looking at things there cannot be any essential difference between a linguistic unit and its meaning or thought it conveys. *sphoṭa* refers to this non-differentiated language principle.[9]

In this context it will be interesting to note how philosophy of mind looks at the issue of language-thought relationship. At certain points it looks like a problem of judging the primacy of either the philosophy of mind or the philosophy of language. When 'thought is presupposed to be analysable in terms of language, philosophers (especially philosophers of language) come out with a general theory of meaning. We have noted in Chapter 3 that Wittgenstein believes that the concepts like 'understanding', 'thought' etc. cannot be judged independent of their use in linguistic communication. Many, like Wittgenstein share the presupposition that a general account of meaning can solve the problems of philosophy of mind. The philosophers of mind would not accept this viewpoint. They would rather like to put emphasis on the independence of analysing the issues concerning the concept of mind, without taking resort to philosphy of language. Collin McGinn in his book *The Character of Mind*, sums up the standpoint of philosophers of mind in the following way :

> But suppose we decided that thoughts were not essentially linguistic: then it would no longer seem right to take a general theory of meaning to be what will put philosophy on the path to the solution of its problems; we shall seek instead a general theory of the content of thought — this being a task for the philosophy of mind. Our proper procedure, on this supposition,

> would be to try to elicit the general principles which govern the way thought acquires its content, and the ways this content gets manifested in judgement and action. . . . Thus on the supposition that thought does not require a linguistic medium and so it is not to be explained in terms of meaning, the philosophy of mind would be methodologically anterior to the philosophy of language — because concepts would be capable of direct investigation.[10]

Bhartṛhari does not face such problem of arguing either for the priority of philosophy of mind or philosophy of language. Such problems are the off-shoot of modern craze for specialisation and fragmentalisation. Nor does he intend to present thought and language as two separate procedures. The basic difference between the modern philosophers of language and Bhartṛhari is that, he looks at the concept of language from two standpoints, i.e., language-in-use, and language as a principle. Both are non-separable yet not identical. Moreover, his philosophical position is holistic in nature.

Before we explicate Bhartṛhari's position on language-thought relationship we must remember that he undertakes the entire issue from the standpoint of communicability of language. So he undertakes a triadic analysis of meaning, where he retains a distinction among language, referents and thought. This distinction is often obliterated in actual practice. For him the study of language involves showing the inter-relationship between the uttered words and thoughts on the one hand, and between the words and referents on the other. It should be noted that most often in the Western philosophy of language (mostly in pre-Wittgensteinian and Wittgensteinian era) the language-referent relationship dominates the show. As a result some philosophers' views the concept of 'thought' and the associated concepts as smacking of a sort of psychologism. The concepts like 'thought', 'idea', 'understanding' are either warded off as Philosophical myths or else as speech-dispositions. Despite such an attitude some modern philosophers have shown interest in language-thought relationship, as is evident from the writings of Quine, Frege, Davidson, Guttenplan and others. Surprisingly enough, Bhartṛhari though a very ancient thinker, took the issue seriously and offered some insightful analysis of the issue.

According to him, whenever we examine language at the level of utterance it must be taken as communicative in nature. But this process of linguistic communication is not explicable exclusively in terms of the speaker and the hearer. We have noted earlier that the process of linguistic transactions poses some peculiar problems. Some of them are as follows :

1. The hearer, in spite of listening carefully to what the speaker has to say fails to understand him.
2. The speaker has no other way but to present his utterance syllable by syllable, each syllable vanishing/dying out, to give place to the utterance of next syllable. Though the hearer listens to each syllable separately, yet he grasps the meaning as one and as a unit.
3. Sometimes, even if the utterance is not completed the hearer understands the complete meaning.
4. Sometimes the speaker gropes for the right word to expresss his intentions and thought.

Such peculiarities at the level of language-in-use shows that analysing language at the level of utterance only is not enough to explicate its communicative nature. There is a need to go beyond this level. Bhartṛhari does this by probing the connection between object-meant/referent and utterance, and further by showing their connection with the ultimate ground of unity amidst thought, language and referent. So thought is presupposed to be a relevant phase of understanding language. The unity of uttered words and ascription of meaning to them involves further unification at the level of thought. This should not be interpreted as indulging in an explication of the psychological process. He rather shows that there is a logical dependence between thought and language. Language needs thought and thought needs language.

I have stated in the chapter on *sphoṭa*, why Bhartṛhari introduces this concept as the ultimate ground of communicability. I need not repeat them here. But it is, atleast, very clearly stated by him that speech and thought are two elements of the same principle. Neither words are reducible to thoughts nor are thoughts reducible to words. Similarly spoken language is not conceived as a copy of thought. Therefore the claim of the philosophers of mind that 'concept' is explainable without reference to their expression in words, does not contradict Bhartṛhari's position as a philosopher of language. Bhartṛhari would say that 'concepts' and 'thoughts' need not be wordy, yet from this it does not follow that it is not **verbally expressible**. We may grope for correct counterpart of thought in the form of words, but that does not preclude the **possibility** of being presented in words. The element of 'thought' and the element of 'utterance', no doubt, are autonomous. But they cannot be autonomous to the extent of being exclusive of each other. No philosopher of mind will deny the fact that one concept is distinct from another, one thought is distinct from another. And this distinction must have a basis. The basis, according to Bhartṛhari is the word-impenetrability. To put it in simpler way, words, and concepts are two sides of the same coin. But we must be cautious enough to observe the subtle distinction between the principle of speech or words as a whole and the particularities of linguistic units used. In this context only the controversy over the primacy either of 'thought' or of 'language', should be solved.

Frege and Davidson on Thought and Language

Against the background of one of the oldest theories of meaning and language, outlined briefly above, it will be quite interesting to compare notes with the views advanced by two modern thinkers, Frege and Davidson on this specific area. I discuss their viewpoints with reference to two of their papers — "Thought — A Logical Inquiry" by Frege and "Thought and Talk" by Davidson. It is to be noted that the thought-language issue, in recent times has gained tremendous importance. Largely as a result of Frege's work it has been brought to the light that some concepts which are necessary to describe language are also an integral part of the description of the mental attitudes. Frege's most significant discovery in the field of philosophy of language is the distinction between the sense and reference. In addition to the name and reference, he adds a third element which he calls the **sense**, which implies the meaning or the descriptive content of the word. So he undertakes a triadic analysis of language in terms of words, referents and sense. This is very akin to Bartṛhari's analysis of language. Frege extends this distinction from the singular and referring expressions to the predicate expressions and to the whole of sentences. He points out that a sentence (which can, at least, be true or false) expresses a **thought**. Frege, in his paper, "The Thought — A Logical Inquiry" makes a detailed analysis of the concept of 'thought'. He says : "I call a thought something for which the question of truth arises. So I ascribe what is false to a thought as much as what is true. So I can say: **thought** is the sense of the sentence without wishing to say as well that the sense of every sentence is a thought. The thought, in itself immaterial, clothes itself in the material garment of a sentence and thereby becomes comprehensible to us. We say a sentence expresses a thought".[11]

It may seem that there is a striking similarity between the Fregean view of language-thought relation and that of Bhartrhari's view on this issue. Yet the difference in their approach to the problem is quite easily detectable. Coming to the points of similarity, we may note that Frege's admission of thought as being immaterial, but comprehensible through the material garment of the uttered speech, points to the similar distinction made by Bhartṛhari between *dhvani* (the verbal and empirical manifestation of language) and *sphoṭa* (the trans-verbal/non-empirical principle of speech). Similarly, while defining thought as immaterial, Frege does not concede to the view that thoughts are subjective 'ideas'. Bhartrhari also does not interpret *madhyamā vāk* in terms of ideas, because he assumes that the intention of the speaker to say something and understanding of the utterance by the hearer are based on the common grasping of the content of speech. But there is a basic difference between Frege and Bhartṛhari's approach. Frege does not start with the assumption that language is communicative in nature and language can have multiple facets. He takes up the analysis of thought to locate the content of the sentences in order to explicate the status of truth. This is evident from his analysis of the phases of thought-language relationship. i.e.,

1. Apprehension of a thought — Thinking
2. Recognition of its truth value — Judgement
3. Manifestation of judgement — Assertion.

Frege makes a distinction between the thought and the assertion of thought. We may however, say that Frege's notion of thought stands for the propositional content, which can be expressed through various sentences and in various languages. So the apprehension of thought may be similar to *paśyantī vāk* of Bhartṛhari. The judgement and assertion may be comparable to the *madhyamā* and *vaikhārī* stage. But this sort of comparison is quite misleading. The concept of truth is the focal point of Frege's thought-language analysis. The conception of 'truth' works as the connecting link between the level of thought and assertion. Consequently, at the level of language, assertions occupy the unique position. Frege excludes imperatives, exclamations, poetics, etc., from the scope of thought.[12] At some points he wants to retain the conceptual autonomy of thought, yet it is the logic of assertion and truth- conditions, which becomes the determining factors of meaning.

Davidson in his paper "Thought and Talk" retains Frege's basic insight but avoids Frege's commitments to 'thought' and truth-values as Platonic entities. Davidson makes further developments on Fregean thesis by modifying Tarski's notion of truth. Regarding thought-language relation, however, he clearly maintains that thought is not a speech-disposition. According to him ". . . the parallel between the structure of thoughts and the structure of sentences provides no argument for the primacy of either, and only a presumption in favour of their interdependence".[13] This is the primary premise from which he concludes that "a creature must be a member of speech community if it is to have a concept of belief. And given the dependence of other attitudes on belief, we can say more generally that a creature that can interpret speech can have the concept of thought".[14] This interpretation, again, seems fairly close to Bhartṛhari's analysis of thought-language relationship. But as we have noticed in case of Frege, Davidson also makes the concept of 'truth' the central point and consequently, he highlights the role of assertions at the level of language. The conception of truth as the key-concept leads to the importance of assertions at the level of language and of belief at the level of thought. So Davidson describes thought as the interlocking system of beliefs which can be held to be true, though he admits that thought can be autonomous in respect of belief. He says " . . .although most of thoughts are not beliefs, it is a pattern of belief that allows us to identify any thought; analogously, in the case of language, although most utterances are not concerned with truth, it is the pattern of sentences held true that gives sentences their meaning".[15] The attitude of holding a sentence to be true relates belief and interpretation (understanding of an utterance) in a fundamental way.

Truth and Belief: The Indian Perspective

So, in case of Frege as well as Davidson the notion of truth has a vital role to play in the explanation of meaning. This obsession with truth and assertion may be due to the fact, as it has been observed by D.M. Datta, that "In English the word knowledge implies a cognition, attended with belief".[16] However, Datta tries to adjust the notion 'belief' in the typical setting of the Indian philosophy of language. He is of the opinion that ". . . a *vākya* (sentence) asserting a fact produces a belief in the fact which forms its objective intention (*tātparya*). A *vākya* comes, therefore, to be a source of knowledge about facts".[17] I, on my part, would prefer to disagree with Datta's interpretation of role of belief and nature of statements in all cases of Indian philosophy of language. Though there is no unanimity of opinion amongst the Indian philosophical schools of thought regarding the nature of language, source of language, the unit of meaning, etc., yet *vākya* is not defined in terms of factual and assertive sentences alone. Nor is belief understood in the sense of objective intention. Imperatives, interrogatives, metaphorical and suggestive use of sentences are also analysed by the Indian Philosophers in the context of *vākya*. John Brough correctly observes that in the West "most of the philosophic discussions of meaning confine itself to a relatively small portion of language behaviour, namely, statements which describe or report a state of affairs — the propositions of the natural sciences, or more generally, such statements as are traditionally handled by logic".[18] This obsession still continues. Though in recent times some philosophers have devoted their attention to the logic of imperatives, aesthetics and other forms of language but an integrated study of language along with its multiple forms of expression is not quite often undertaken. Wittgenstein in his *Philosophical Investigations* highlights this multiplicity of linguistic uses and reacts against Fregean analysis of language in terms of truth. But his non-essentialistic stance makes him concentrate more on the function of the language than on the explorations of its structural basis. In post-Wittgensteinian era communication-intention theorists, have made further examinations of the basic concepts of communication, viz., the pragmatics of language, the role of intention, belief, the speaker-hearer relationship, etc. But by doing this, they have most often concentrated on the level of uttered speech. Here Bhartṛhari seems to score over the non-essentialists in the sense that he not only examines the language at the level of the uttered speech but probes deeper to bring out the ultimate logical ground of meaning. He elaborates with equal zest the role of usage, convention, syntax, speaker-hearer relationship, the context of the speech, when he analyses language at the level of the verbal manifestations or speech. But he at the same time, is of the opinion that we must go beyond the level of the uttered speech to find out how the meaning is conveyed in spite of the variations in the form of language adopted and the peculiarities of the speaker. I feel, Frege as well as Davidson are also in search of this ultimate basis of meaningfulness, which I propose to take up in the concluding part of this chapter. But for the time being our problem is; can we fit the Indian notion of language in the model of assertions ?

Professor Datta in order to show that in the Indian Philosophy of Language the role of belief and truth are equally accepted, tries to highlight that the two of the conditions of meaningful sentences admitted by some schools of Indian philosophy, atleast, refer to belief and truth-conditions. The *Nyāya*, *Mīmāṁsā*, *Vedānta* schools of philosophy accept four conditions for the meaningfulness of the *vākya* (sentence); they are — *akāṅkṣā* (syntactic expectancy) *yogyatā* (logical compatibility) *sannidhi* (phonetic contiguity) and *tātparya* (context or the general purport of the sentence). According to Datta *tātparya* refers to the belief of the speaker. But other interpreters explain *tātparya* as the intention of the speaker. In fact, *tātparya* is more a part of hearer's understanding than the speaker's meaning. Even if, in the broad sense of term, *tātparya* is taken as implying speaker's intention then also 'intention' and 'belief' are not identical concepts. They have different implications. So *tātparya* does not refer to 'belief' at all. Similarly *yogyatā*, in the true sense of the term, does not mean "compatibility with facts", as it has been interpreted by Datta. K.K. Raja correctly observes : "It is necessary to distinguish between inconceivable combinations like 'the circular square' and the conceivable combinations which are against our experience such as 'the rabit's horn'. Strictly speaking it is the inconceivability of mutual association of word-meanings that renders the whole sentence non-sensical; it is not the lack of correlation with the actual facts, but impossibility of connecting the word-meanings that stands in the way of verbal comprehension".[19] So neither the concept of 'belief' is accepted as one of the conditions of knowing the sentence-meaning nor the factual statements (the compatibility with facts) are the only type of statements. In case of Bhartṛhari, the role of belief is not emphasised for he holds that the content of speech is not transmitted by the speaker to the hearer, rather the spoken words serve as a stimulus to reveal the meaning which is already present in the mind of the hearer.

Bhartṛhari strongly holds that it is the sentence which is the primary unit of meaningful speech. There is certain self-sufficiency and completeness about its expressive capacity when the meaning is understood along with the intention of the speaker. For the expression, as well as for understanding of a meaningful statement, at a terpretation of the truth-value of the assertion is not called for. In Bhartṛhari's conception of language, the concept of 'truth' does not come in between the utterance and meaningfulness. Moreover, at a linguistic level he does not confine his analysis to **assertions** only. I do admit that both Frege and Davidson accept that language can have other uses too. But they prefer to concentrate on the logic of assertions. This may be convenient for the Formalistic explanation of language. But when language is viewed as a communicative phenomenon, one may find that 'language' as a concept is much more complicated. And excavating the logic of language through the concepts of 'belief' and 'truth' do not solve the problem. The basic approach to the language-thought relation in case of Bhartṛhari is different from that of Frege and Davidson. Bhartṛhari explains 'thought' and 'language' from the standpoint of communicability. But Frege does not proceed with the assumption that language is primarily communicative in nature. He makes a distinction between the 'thought' and 'language' to show the distinction between the propositional content and the sentence. Davidson on the other hand, tries to locate the counterpart of assertions at the level of thought to locate the propositional attitudes that are accompanied by sentences like 'I believe', 'I feel'. 'I think', 'I doubt' etc., which he does ultimately in terms of belief.

Search for the Ultimate Ground of Communication

Our problem does not end with showing the difference of approach to the problem of language-thought relationship as envisaged by Bhartṛhari on the one hand, and Frege and Davidson on the other. It will not be too much out of context to say that both Frege and Davidson are in search of the logical ground of meaning, as has been done by Bhartṛhari. This logical ground can be located in the concept of 'thought' in case of Frege and concept of 'interpretation' in case of Davidson.

Frege holds that 'thought' "belongs neither to my inner world as an idea nor yet to the outer world of material, perceptual things".[20] So "Thoughts are by no means unreal but their reality is of a quite different kind from that of things. And their effect is brought about by an act of the thinker without which they would be ineffective, at least as far as we can see. And yet the thinker does not create them but must take them as they are. They can be true without being apprehended by a thinker and are not wholly unreal even then, at least if they could apprehended and by this means be bought into operation".[21]

This sort of explanation of the concept of 'thought' comes closer to the concept of *sphoṭa*, the ultimate ground of meaning unaffected by the speaker and the objects of the world. For Frege 'thought' implies 'truth' self-evident in the sense that "It is not true for the first time when it is discovered, but is like a planet which, already before anyone has seen it, has been in interaction with other planets".[22] The word 'true' is used here by Frege definitely in a different sense than it has been used as a characteristic of assertion. Here thought stands for the logical ground of language and meaning. Is not Frege's description of 'thought' approximating Bhartṛhari's concept of *sphoṭa* which is self-expressive and self-valid? Frege further observes, "one sees a thing, one has an idea, one apprehends or thinks a thought. When one apprehends or thinks a thought one does not create it but only comes to stand in a certain relation, which is different from seeing a thing or having an idea, to what already existed before-hand".[23]

Bhartrhai conceives *sphoṭa*, also, as the meaning-whole or the implicit principle of meaning neither definable in terms of objects nor in terms of the words used. Here I do not intend to claim that Frege offers us nothing original and that it has already been anticipated by Bhartṛhari. I have already indicated the differences of their approach to the problem of language. But once language is analysed at its depth level it is apt to direct us towards some sort of unity, which Frege locates in the concept of 'thought', whereas Bhartṛhari conceives it through the assumption of the concept of *sphoṭa*.

Davidson, while trying to do away with Frege's entitative commitment to 'thought' advances the theory of interpretation. He says, "we usually think that having a language consists largely in being able to speak, but in what follows speaking will play an indirect part, what is essential to my argument is the idea of an interpreter, someone who understands the utterances of another".[24] Here is a thesis which explains both thought and speech in terms of interpretability. But what is the gound of interpretation ? Davidson's answer is that the method of interpretation "puts the interpreter in general agreement with the speaker, according to the method the speaker holds the sentence true under specified conditions, and these conditions obtain, in the opinion of the interpreter, just when the speaker holds the sentences to be true".[25] So for Davidson, ultimately holding a belief to be true is the central point of interpretation. But on what ground does the interpreter judge an utterance to be true ? Is it because of its relation to the facts and referents ? Davidson again clarifies, "this notion of truth is not a semantical notion: language is not directly in picture . . . . it is a part of the frame. For the notion of a true belief depends on the notion of a true utterance, and this in turn cannot be without a shared-language".[26] So from the notion of interpretation he comes to the concept of truth to return again to interpretation in terms of a 'shared language'. The speaker and hearer communicate because they are interpreters of meaning in terms of 'truth'. And this is made possible on the assumption of a 'shared-language'. In any case, it seems that we cannot escape the concept of a common and universal ground of meaning, if language is to be interpreted in terms of communicability.

References

1. K.K. Raja, *Indian Theories of Meaning*, Adyar Library and Research Centre, Madras, p. 3.
2. Strawson, *Analysis and Metaphysics*, p. 96.
3. B.K. Matilal, *The Word and the World*, p. 135.
4. *na sā chaitanye nāvisthā jātirasti yasyā* |
   svaparaṃ sambvodho yo vacā nānugamyate, ||
   (*Vāk.*, 1.8)
5. *yo'yaṃ caitanye vāgrupatānugamastena* |
   loke sasamjño visamjñā iti vyapadeśaḥ kṛiyate, ||
   (*Vāk.*, p. 193. 1.3. (K.S. Iyer))

6. Wilfrid Sellars, "Conceptual Change", In *Conceptual Change*, ed. by D. Pearce and P. Maynard, Dordrecht, 1973, p. 82.
7. Donald Davidson, "Thought and Talk", In *Mind and Language*, ed. by S.D. Guttenplan, Oxford, Clarendon Press, 1976, p. 7.
8. Matilal, *The Word and the World*, p. 137.
9. *Ibid.*, p. 85.
10. Collin McGinn, *The Character of Mind*, Oxford University Press, 1982, pp. 124-25.
11. G. Frege, *The Thought: A Logical Inquiry*, p. 20.
12. *Ibid.*, p. 21 and 22.
13. D. Davidson, *Thought and Talk*, p. 10.
14. *Ibid.*
15. *Ibid.*, p. 14.
16. D.M. Datta, *Six Ways of Knowing*, University of Calcutta, 1972, p. 19.
17. *Ibid.*, p. 332.
18. John Brough, *Some Indian Theories of Meaning*, p. 176.
19. K.K. Raja, *Indian Theories of Meaning*, p. 165.
20. G. Frege, *Thought*, p. 35.
21. *Ibid.*, p. 38.
22. *Ibid.*, p. 29.
23. *Ibid.*, p. 29-30n.
24. Davidson, *Thought and Talk*, p. 9.
25. *Ibid.*, p. 9.
26. *Ibid.*, p. 21.

7

The Word and the World

Semantics and Ontology

In the previous chapter I have hinted at Bhartṛhari's triadic analysis of language. This involves an explication of two-fold relationship, i.e., the relation between word and thought, and the relation between word and the world (referent). I have already dwelt on Bhartṛhari's conception of word-thought relationship. Now I will like to take up for discussion the word-referent relationship. This issue is more complicated in nature, for most often this epistemic issue tends to turn into an ontological one. We generally believe that words mean the things. In other words, we use language to describe the existent reality. So meaning has commonly been conceived as a function of 'naming'. It is a sort of naming the referent or the object-meant. But this is not the end of what we conceive regarding word-world relationship. Discussions on the nature of the relationship often boils down to the question on 'what there is?'. In fact, it sometimes appears that there is a two-way relationship between semantics and ontology. For often the philosophers tend to believe that the problem of explaining the nature of the world can be better solved by probing into the nature of 'what do we do with words' ? As Quine puts it, "It is no wonder, then, that ontological controversy should end into controversy over language".[1] Therefore, we note that there is a subtle connection between the theory of meaning and the theory of existence, even though theoretically they belong to two separate areas of study. The semantical analysis of language is supposed to be confined to the explication of relation between the word and referent or facts. One can confine oneself within the strict boundaries of such an analysis if he is involved in the semantics of *formal* language. But when it is about the natural language, even the most rigorous form of semantics implicitly suggests some ontological commitments. And most often it over-reaches its boundary to trespass into the area of ontology. This tendency is natural. The philosopher's conception of the world and its status often determines how the word should relate itself to the world of objects and events. While discussing Bhartṛhari's world-view in Chapter 2. I have explicitly stated about his phenomenalistic stand. His world-view, naturally, influences his notion of semantics.

Bhartṛhari maintains that there is a close relationship between the word and what is meant by the word. It has already noted earlier (in Chapter 4) that he describes the relationship in terms of *samjñā* and *samjñīn*. In most of the standard books on Bhartṛhari, these two terms are translated as 'name' and the 'named'. But I feel the translation of *samjñā* as 'name', may present certain difficulties, especially, for those who are acquainted with the Western theories of meaning. *Samjñā* in a broad sense also implies a concept or an idea that we form about the use of a term. *Samjñā* stands for the definition of a word. It will be convenient for us, in the present context, to use the term in the above sense. This will help us to present Bhartṛhari's views in clearer terms.

The definition of meaning as a function of 'naming' implies that words stand for 'names'. The term 'name' often holds the philosophers captive of a sort of picture-thinking (to use Wittgenstein's phrase). The use of the term 'name' suggests the picture of a corresponding object 'named'. There are some words which have their objective counter part in the world. But the word 'pegasus' does not correspond to an existing entity in space and time. Still the picture of 'name and the named' leads some philosophers to conceive of a 'mental entity' nontheless existent, i.e., existent in a different sense. Russell exploded the myth by very rightly pointing out that the so-called singular descriptions using names can be used without supposing that there might be such entities. But Russell's theory is more about the definite descriptions than about names. Rather Frege is more explicit when he shows that there cannot be one-to-one relationship between the word (name) and the referent (named). 'Morning star' and 'evening star' are two different word-compounds implying two different meanings yet having one referent. In this case one referent is described in two ways. From this it becomes clear that the use of the word 'name' has duped the philosophers in the past. So it is better for us to avoid the term 'name' in explaining Bhartṛhari's word-referent relationship. He never has conceived words in that sense, because he clearly states with examples (as cited earlier) that there are many words without any objective referent.

In case of Bhartṛhari *saṃjñā* and *saṃjñīn* relationship can be best described as a relationship between definition and definiendum. In fact, Bhartṛhari would say, we use words to describe or to express. But what we describe or express need not be about objects. We have some sort of compulsion of thinking about the objects as the things-meant if we take words to be the ultimate unit of meaning. Bhartṛhari has no such compulsion, for he attributess primacy to sentence-meaning, not to word-meaning. Besides, he believes that primary meaning of any referential word is the universal, not particular. And lastly, according to him both the *saṃjñā* and *saṃjñīn* are linguistic in nature. The object referred to is not originally extra-linguistic. The last two ideas cited above will become clear as we proceed with Bhartṛhari's theory of word-world relationship.

Sometime back I had hinted at the relation between semantics and ontology. I had also pointed out that the ontological scheme of a philosopher has its bearing on his conception of word-world relationship. Let us therefore examine Bhartṛhari's ontological status. In Indian context we may broadly pin-point three types of rival ontologies. They are — Realism, Atomism and Holism. The *Nyāya -Vaiśeṣika* offers a realistic world-view according to which the world is populated by real particulars, universals and relations. So when we talk of a 'table' it refers to an existing table out there in the space and time. Buddhists, especially Diṇṇāga envisages the world to be populated by momentary particulars (*svalakṣaṇas*). They are not nameable. Our words which describe objects are not adequate enough to catch within its net the true nature of the momentary and structureless particulars. So concepts and words are linguistic constructs (*vikalpa*). The third type of ontology is offered by Bhartṛhari. It is Holistic. According to him, the reality is undifferentiated and unanalysable whole. But in our thought and language, we are in habit of cutting bits and pieces out of this whole reality and assigning them a 'metaphorical existence'. The real word is beyond our grasp. Our words (also word-impregnated concepts) are mental constructs (*kalpanā*) or linguistic constructs (*vikalpa*). In other words, our language does not and cannot refer to the objects or real referents. The last two views about the world (objects) and the language are radically different from the *Nyāya-Vaiśeṣika* Realism. The notion of the word/language in relation to the world is developed in different ways by Diṇṇāga and Bhartṛhari. Yet it is interesting to note that they share a certain degree of common semantical notion. In view of such similarities I intend to make a comparative analysis of Bhartṛhari's and Diṇṇāga's views on the topic. It may help us in revealing an interesting aspect of philosophy of language as a whole. It is interesting, because here is the case of two philosophers whose rival ontological views lead them to a common converging point in semantics.

It is well-known that Diṇṇāga quotes some crucial passages from Bhartṛhari's *Vākyapadīya* in his treatise *Pramāṇasamuccaya* [2] to vindicate his own views. On the basis of this evidence it can be claimed that there are subtle shades of similarity between *sphoṭa* theory of meaning, and the *apoha* theory of meaning propagated by Diṇṇāga. Yet the moment we try to analyse their respective philosophies we become aware of the vast range of differences between them. They adopt divergent approaches in their handling of metaphysical and epistemological issues. For Bhartṛhari *śabda* is a primary form of *pramāṇa*, where as for Diṇṇāga *śabda* does not have even an independent status as a *pramāṇa*. This makes our task of tracing similarities more interesting. To do full justice to the task in hand, I need to dwell briefly on the metaphysical and epistemological background of both these philosophers. We must start by highlighting the points of difference till we reach the point of convergence.

I need not discuss much about Bhartṛhari's position. We have discussed them earlier. But while summing up his position it can be said that he is a Monist in his metaphysical stance and his world-view is Holistic. And in his epistemology he offers primacy to *śabda*. In other words, it is a form of Pan-verbalism, which explains all forms of knowledge and cognition in terms of 'word-loadedness'. In Bhartṛhari's conceptual scheme 'unity' is the key-word. It alone is primary and real.

The Buddhist (Diṇṇāga's) Viewpoint

Diṇṇāga, on the other hand, in true Buddhist tradition, denies the status of unity, whole and eternity. His metaphysical position is pluralistic and atomistic. But his pluralism is logical in nature. He conceives the ultimate Reality as unique particulars, which are known as *svalakṣaṇas.* They are no ordinary particulars, i.e., objects or things, but a series of fleeting moments and point-instants. They are devoid of any characterisation, nor are they locatable in space and time. Yet these *svalakṣaṇas* or 'the essence of their own being', are independent of our mind. They are cognisable because they are perceivable. Diṇṇāga describes *svalakṣaṇa* in the following manner: "The perception of sense-perception is *rūpa* (i.e., that belongs to the sensory faculty) which is cognisable simply as it is and which is **inexpressible**" (*Pramāṇasamuccaya,* Ch.I., Verse 5. ed). In other words, they are simple, unanalysable units perceivable but not conceivable. This sort of atomistic stand by Diṇṇāga stems from Buddha's famous pronouncement : "One sees blue, but one does not see 'It is blue'.'' The moment one says 'It is blue' he objectivises the fleeting moments. Objects occupy space and time and they have some amount of stability and continuity in existence. But *svalakṣaṇas* cannot be understood with reference to space, time and stability. They are existent not in ordinary sense but in a logical sense. The moment we try to talk about them we objectivise them by attaching names and concepts to them. So the ideas of objects and things occur when the pure percepts are confused with the mental categories and concepts. Concepts are the products of mind. So any kind of conceptualisation involves projection through imagination (*kalpanā*) and mental construction (*vikalpa*). Concepts present a unified picture of what is particular. Therefore *svalakṣaṇas* (the ultimately Real) is inconceivable and unutterable.

This sort of metaphysical atomism has its ramifications in his theory of epistemology. Unlike, Bhartṛhari, he believes that there can be concept-free cognition and awareness. Diṇṇāga specifies that there are two sources of knowledge, i.e., percept and concept. Percept is the direct source of knowledge, whereas concept is indirect. Epistemologically, percept and sense-awareness precede concepts. The former is the means of cognising the unconditioned and ultimate Reality, i.e., *svalakṣaṇas,* whereas the latter leads to the knowledge of the conditioned Reality. However, when we take recourse to expressing our awareness and experience through language, we have no way but to take help from the faculty of concepts. All linguistic expressions are done through the mode of conceptualisation, and this in turn, are a form of universalisation. So the unique and particularised reality cannot be grasped by the concepts in its true nature.

So far we have been concentrating on the contrasting characteristics of Bhartṛhari's and Diṇṇāga's metaphysical and epistemological background. Let us now have a look at their semantic position. The central issue of semantics is — how to relate the word with the world. It is a common belief that language has, primarily, a referring role, i.e., words must denote the things and events of the world. This belief arises because we want to bridge the epistemic gulf between the subject and object of knowledge, between the knower and the known. So it is taken for granted that the knower is the possessor of language and concepts; and concepts must refer to objects. The issue is crystallised in the form "what does the word refer to ?" The obvious answer is — 'Object'. When one says 'cow' it refers to the object cow. But how do we know that the object is a cow ? To call some object a 'cow' one must classify the object as belonging to the class 'cow', for the same word can be used to refer to similar objects as cows. However, classification is a form of universalisation. Universalisation, in turn leads to concept formation. So the referring role of words requires conceptualisation and universalisation. On this issue few philosopers would disagree. So the problem acquires a new form, i.e., do we conceptualise and classify on the basis of real universal qualities present in the objects of a class ? To put it more articulately — are the universals mind-dependent or object-dependent ? The Realists like *Nyāya-Vaiśeṣikas* will say that universals are real and object-dependent. For them, universal is as real as the particular. The particular, qualified by the universal, constitutes the true denotation of a word. They define the universal (*jāti*) as that which exists in the different particulars of the same species. This makes the application of the same name to different particulars of the same class possible. But Diṇṇāga and Bhartṛhari, take the opposite stand. According to them universal is a mental category. We see the objects as qualified by universal qualities because our mind projects them in that way. The philosophical position of these two thinkers is a radical departure from the prevalent Realism of their time. This Mentalistic and

Nominalistic stand, at the outset may appear to be implausible and unsound. But they both offer sufficient logical justification for this novel way of interpreting the concept of universal.

Bhartṛhari and Diṇṇāga on Word-World Relation

We have noted earlier that Diṇṇāga's and Bhartṛhari's ontological positions are widely divergent. Bhartṛhari's Pan-linguism and Holism is in direct contrast with Diṇṇāga's Linguistic Phenomenalism; again the former's monism is contrary to the latter's atomism and pluralism. Yet in the matters of semantics they agree on some crucially important points. They are : (1) no application of word is possible without universalisation, (2) the thing-meant or object-denoted cannot be known directly through words, (3) universals are mind-dependent, (4) universalisation and conceptualisation necessarily involve differentiation and negation. Let us now examine how both these thinkers expound their views in this area of study.

Bhartṛhari's entire attitude towards the word-object relationship is guided by Patanjali's crucial remark : "We are the linguist analysts, for us what word says is our guide". Bhartṛhari further elaborates this as "what is the use of our reflecting on the nature of things ? The object is for us what the word presents". One may note the direct influence of this attitude when he comes down to the analysis of relationship between the form of the word (*grāhya*) and what a word conveys or denotes (*grāhaka*); and the relationship between the name or words (*samjñā*) and named (*samjñīn*). He specifically points out that we cannot refer to the objects directly without referring to the form of the word. Unless and until the form of the word is understood meaning remains uncommunicated. So words primarily refer to the *vācya* or the form of the word. From this it follows that *grāhya* and *grāhaka*; and *samjñā* and *samjñīn* are identical. At the level of utterance when we make differentiation, we can at best directly refer to the level of **words** not the **world**. He admits that words are, of course, used to denote objects or facts. But in all such cases, the object-meant is grasped by the hearer's awareness and then it is transferred to the objects-meant. According to Bhartṛhari, every word is a concept and hence is universal. So each word at the outset refers to the universal of the word and then it is superimposed (*adhyāropakalpanā*) on the universal of the thing-meant (*V.P.,* III.1.6). The meaning of a word cannot be an object or substance-meant, but a mental construct (*vikalpa*) produced in us of the object (*V.P.*, III.1.9.). So the object-as-such is never captured by the words. This is because an object can be described in innumerable ways: for example, a man may be referred to as 'father', 'farmer' etc. The concept referring to the object represents how and under what guise it is captured by our mind. So he calls these referential words as *vikalpa*. This is determinate in nature. They are word-generated. Yet such word-generated concepts are not private and subjective. They are shared by all conscious beings, because that is how language works.

Now the question arises that even if these referent or objects are word-generated, what should be their true nature ? Does the word refer (even indirectly) to the objective universals ? In other words can there be objective universals corresponding to the mental category of universals ? The Realists like *Nyāya* may argue that even if all universals are not object-dependent, atleast, some are. They are out there in the world, and because particulars share a specific universal essence they are cognised as belonging to that class. For example, a particular object is called a 'cow' because the universal essence of 'cowhood' is really present in the object. Bhartṛhari, however would not agree with such a conception of universal. He brings out to our notice certain subtle nuances of the concept of universal, neglected by the Realists. The Realists explain 'universal' in terms of object-universal (*arthajāti*). Bhartṛhari on the other hand shows that the concept of object-universal is not fully explicable without reference to the word-universal (*śabdajāti*). If the basis of the use of the word 'cow' is 'cowhood', Bhartṛhari argues, then what is the basis of the term 'cowhood' itself ? If we follow the Realist's line of thought then we will be compelled to accept that there is another thing-universal for the term 'cowhood' and so on *ad infinitum*. Therefore, the Realists, like *Nyāya,* do not admit that there can be a universal in universal. But paradox cannot be ignored so easily. Here Bhartṛhari comes forward with the solution with the introduction of the concept of word-universal (*śabdajāti*). He argues that "not only could the 'basis' or 'ground' for using a name be a universal, but also uniform basis of application of names to varying things deserve a uniform 'basis' or 'ground' of application and usage".[3] He also offers two very crucial arguments in support of his thesis of word-universal. First, if varying particulars are themselves made the basis for using a class name on the ground that they share a common-essence, then the problem of innumerability (*ananta*) would arise. Learning a name like 'cow' and what it means will be difficult, for there are innumerable number of cows (including past, present and future cows). How can one know what the universal 'cowhood' refers to without knowing all particulars and the essence they share ? So it is safer to start with word-universal and once we know what the word 'cowhood' as a term means then one can apply the term to innumerable cases on the basis of the word-universal. Secondly, if we believe that universals are present in the object we may face the problem of variability (*vyabhicāra*). The particulars in connection with which we learn a name and the vast cases to which the term is applied, may vary. So Bhartṛhari puts forward the thesis that words, first of all, mean the word-universal and thereafter superimposes (*śabdādhyāropa*) them on thing-universal. The identification or rather the confusion between *śabdajāti*/word-universal and *arthajāti*/thing-universal can be compared to the case of a crystal reflecting the redness of a flower placed near it. In such a case one may say that the crystal is red though it is due to the false identification of the reflection of redness with the actual colour of the crystal.

From the above explanation it should not be concluded that Bhartṛhari is a hard-core Nominalist, who interprets the objective world as a mental projection or *kalpanā*. His position is more Phenomenalistic than Nominalistic. He only says that the real nature of thing-as-such cannot be shown by our words. The things/objects that we refer to by the use of words are determined by how we define the word-universal. They are limited by mind-dependent attributes and qualities. The real-existence understood through words is determinate (*savikalpaka*). The real-existence as such is beyond verbal penetration. He calls this sort existence *mukhya-sattā*, which is unutterable and indeterminate (*nirvikalpaka*). The existence that is presented through language has a secondary status. This is called *upacāra sattā*, which can be translated as 'metaphorical' existence. In a metaphor we superimpose the qualities of one object on another: for example, "This boy is a lion". We understand the meaning of the statement by attributing the characteristics of lion such as bravery and ferociousness, to the boy. In Reality a boy cannot be a lion. Similarly the reality as-such, according to Bhartrhari, is not expressible in language. The elements of uttered speech, i.e., the differentiation between word, referent and meaning is not there at the level of ultimate Reality, but is superimposed on it when we describe it through language.

This leads us to realise that, according to Bhartṛhari, conceptualisation is a way of determination and limitation (*upādhi*). It necessarily involves the process of differentiation (*bhedya*). So he makes it clear that, "A universal property is that property common to all members of a class which distinguishes a particular member of that class from non-members. Or some say, the general feature (*ākṛti*) is that which is spoken of as common, and again it is spoken of as a particular substance (*dravya*) to indicate differentiation. But differentiation and identity require limitation, by something other (than the things differentiated or identified)".[4] In other words, he implicitly states that each word implies the negation of its contrary. It involves the process of assertion and negation. Bhartṛhari's way of interpreting word-universal and word-object relationship seems to have strong influence on Diṇṇāga. Bhartṛhari was the elder contemporary of Diṇṇāga. His indebtedness can be noted in his work, *Pramāṇasamuccaya* (*vṛttis* on *Apohapariccheda*). Especially *Jātisamuddeśa* of *Vākyapadīya* III plays a very important role in the formation of his theory of *apoha*. He quotes Bhartṛhari to support the argument that a universal word (*jāti-śabda*) can be directly applied to universals; and to support the argument that a universal word may never be applied directly to the another universal.[5] Though some authentic books on Diṇṇāga like *Buddhist Logic* by Stcherbatsky do not mention anything about this, some later writers like K. Kunjunni Raja, B.K. Matilal, Massaki Hattori give sufficient hints about the strange similarity of views between Bhartṛhari and Diṇṇāga in the matters of language analysis. Here I shall discuss in brief Diṇṇāga's views on universal and word-object relationship to expound the subtle points of similarity.

Diṇṇāga maintains that words cannot directly refer to objects. What we call objects are the products of conceptualisation. For word is the source of concept and concept is the source of word (*vikalpa yonaya śabdaḥ vikalpa śabda yonayaḥ*).[6] Conceptualisation, on the other hand, is not possible without the use of universals. The so-called objects or things-meant are unreal in nature. For Reality is plurality of moments or point-instants (*svalakṣaṇas*). They can be perceived but not conceived. They are indeterminate (*nirvikalpaka*). Diṇṇāga calls them things-as-such (or rather moments-as-such).

And they alone are ultimately Real Beings (*paramārtha sat*). What we project as objects and referents are empirically real (*saṃvṛtti sat*). The 'given' or the 'reality' which are referred to through our language are concept-dependent. One may note here the similarity of distinction between Bhartṛhari's *mukhya sattā* and *upacāra sattā* and Diṇṇāga's *paramārtha Sat* and *Samvṛtti Sat.* Both maintain that the world-as-such or Reality-as-such is **unutterable**. What is utterable is the phenomenal reality. The only metaphysical difference being, that for Bhartṛhari the ultimate Reality is **one Brahman**, and for Diṇṇāga this is the **plurality** of *svalakṣaṇas.* But this opposite metaphysical stance does not affect their semantical position. Both are phenomenalists in this respect. Diṇṇāga's Phenomenalistic position does not allow him to accept universal as real and object-dependent. He argues out how a common essence can be shared by a particular object, because particular objects themselves are mentally constructed out of dissimilar unique particulars (*svalakṣaṇas*). So the concept of a real universal (*jāti/sāmānya*) is replaced by the concept of names and mental constructs (*śabda-vikalpa*). The universals are mere names (*samjñā-mātram*); they are mere concepts without the external reality serving as their basis (*vastuśūnya vikalpa*). So Diṇṇāga holds that universality is purely mental in nature which is converted into external objects through words. "And such are the habits of thought of common humanity that they believe this projection to represent a real universal".[7] "This projection-dispersion of things entirely residing in the intellect, as if they were external, is settled by the cognizer, according to his manner of thinking, as a universal".[8] So names do not represent a real-universal. The theory that names represent the real universal is rejected on the ground of 'infinity and discrepancy' (*ānantyād vyabhicarāc ca*).[9] These two arguments are almost similar to Bhartṛhari's arguments, discussed in this chapter earlier. B.K. Matilal points out that Bhartṛhari's arguments are "fully absorbed by Diṇṇāga who propounded his theory of *apoha* or 'exclusion' as word-meanings rejecting the reality of thing-universals or phenomenal universals".[10] The concept of *vikalpa* or the mental construct refers to the *śabdajāti* through which he explains the concept of names and classes. He explains the term *vikalpa* as *dvābidhi,* i.e., the bifurcation of consciousness into subject and object (*grāhya-grāhakatva vikalpa*).[11] One may, again, note convergence of views of both Diṇṇāga and Bhartṛhari. Bhartṛhari also shows the bifurcation between the word and the object-denoted as mental and word-generated. Like Bhartṛhari, Diṇṇāga too, believes that not only universals but other categories like particulars, substance, etc., are the products of linguistic usage and hence conceptual constructs.[12]

Diṇṇāga's conception of universal and concepts ultimately lead us to his famous theory of *apoha*. The theory implies that "to mean is to exclude". Whenever we use words to mean anything we use the category of universal on the basis of certain functional property. To define the boundary of what it includes one must know what it excludes. Universalisation means negation of counter-positive. Whenever we mean anything by 'cow' we also mean that it excludes from its meaning all 'non-cows'. Differentiation is the means to unity. In case of universalisation we bring dissimilar objects under one unitary class on the basis of differentiating and excluding the functional properties other than the property which serves as the basis of unification. It is unfortunate, that some of his contemporaries branded it as a theory of negative judgement. But it is sheer misrepresentation of a logically sound theory. As Jinendrabuddhi in his commentary on Diṇṇāga's *Pramāṇasamuccaya* points out "our opponents are ignorant of the real essence of the Negative Meaning of words. They impute us (a theory which we never professed)".[13]

Understanding of words and concepts through the logic of exclusion can be possible if one adopts a Linguistic Phenomenalism. Both Bhartṛhari and Diṇṇāga believe that the explication of the concept of meaning is not possible without applying the notions of determination through exclusion. It is not possible to adopt such a theory without accepting the concept of word-universal. The word-universals alone can be negated and excluded not the thing-universal. For this will lead to self-contradiction, as existent thing cannot be both positive and negative in nature.

Linguistic Phenomenalism : An Assessment

From our discussions above it becomes largely clear that, both, Diṇṇāga and Bhartṛhari share a common platform regarding word-object relationship. Both adopt a sort of Linguistic Phenomenalism in the matters of semantics. Now let us assess the logical plausibility of such an unusual approach to the issue. At first sight, it may appear that they are making the semantic analysis unnecessarily cumbersome and complicated. It also seems to militate against the commonsensical and general understanding of the problem of semantics. But a little probe will show that the Linguistic Phenomenalism of Bhartṛhari and Diṇṇāga are better equipped to solve certain ticklish issues associated with word-object relationship.

We use language to communicate our thought. But we should note that language is not always used to refer to and designate objects of the world. Linguistic usage has multiple dimensions. It can be used to mean matters concerning morality, emotions, aesthetics, religion, etc. And in all cases there are no corresponding objects out in the world. Bhartṛhari very rightly cites the example of words like "wheel of fire", "sky flower" etc. Nowhere in the empirical world such objects exist. This peculiarity of language has forced the later *Nyāya* to make a distinction between real universal (*jāti*) and nominal universal (*upādhi*). But the problem does not end there. Two more important difficulties are pointed out by Bhartṛhari. First, most of our linguistic expressions are judgemental in nature. So the subject or the substance is related to quality, action, number etc. If we follow the Realistic logic then they are real and object-dependent. In a judgement the subject and predicate are to be related, for example, "The table is red". Here the concept 'table' and 'red' are said to have a relation. The relation, according to the Realists, is a real and objective category. Bhartṛhari points out that to explain the relationship between the subject and predicate one has to presume a further relationship between the concept of 'relationship' and the actual relationship, and so on *ad infinitum*. Bhartṛhari and Diṇṇāga get out of this 'paradox' by understanding empirical facts in terms of conceptual constructs and *sabdajāti*. Secondly, if language is judgemental then most of the sentences either assert or negate facts. If one follows the Realistic logic then it would be difficult to explain the negative propositions, such as "the tree does not exist". According to the Realists the term 'tree' denotes a real object tree. So the moment 'tree' is uttered it is implied that tree is existent. But how can we say "tree does not exist", for by saying "does not exist" in the predicate we are negating a primary being denoted by the term 'tree' ? How can an object exist and not exist at the same time ? This will be a contradiction. Similarly, in case of an assertion, such as "the tree exists", the predicate 'exists' is redundant because the term 'tree' itself implies an existing tree. So the statement becomes tautological.[14] These arguments of Bhartṛhari are repeated by the Buddhists.[15] Such logically ticklish issues can be resolved if one agrees with Bhartṛhari and Diṇṇāga that words do not refer directly to the objects and relations, but to the words and conceptual constructs (*vikalpas*).

The problem of conceiving language in primarily a referential role has always created metaphysical tangles for the philosophers in the East as well as the West. Plato conceived words as universals, but believed that universals are real. The world being unreal the real universals 'subsist' in the mystical 'other world'. Aristotle demystified it, but still believed that universals are real and objective. The tradition was followed by Mill and Meinong. However, the problem takes a new turn in the recent century. The referential model in essence is retained, but instead of believing that words denote objects it is stated that the propositions or statements refer not to the objects but to states-of-affairs or to events. Early Wittgenstein, Frege, Russell contributed to this Referential theory of meaning. This has resulted in attaching primacy to assertions and negations in the scheme of linguistic expressions. It is only after later Wittgenstein pointed out that language is not primarily referential in nature that philosophers started becoming aware of the multiple dimensions of meaning-analysis. Yet one cannot say that philosophers of our time have totally got rid of the 'dogma of reference'. It seems that Bhartṛhari and Diṇṇāga could avoid the dogma and the problems associated with it because of their Linguistic Phenomenalism. One can say that they are not bewitched by the designative role of language because Bhartṛhari is primarily a *śabdapramāṇaka*, i.e., linguistic analyst and Diṇṇāga is primarily a logician. And, as is well-known, neither the language analyst nor the logician have anything to do with the existence and non-existence of empirical facts. Therefore, both aim at defining 'semantic' categories, such as universal and substance, whereas the Realists like *Vaiśeṣika* and *Nyāya* take resort to 'ontology' in their analysis of language.[16]

References

1. W.V.O. Quine, *From a Logical Point of View*, Harvard University Press, 1953, p. 16.
2. K. Potter, *Encyclopaedia of Indian Philosophies*, Vol. V., p. 28. Diṇṇāga quotes *Vāk*, III.14.8, II.158, II.155.

3. B.K. Matilal, *The Word and the World*, p. 85.
4. *Ibid.*, p. 37.
5. *Vākyapadīya*, III.I.14-24. As summarised by A. Aklujkar in *Encyclopaedia of Indian Philosophies*, Vol. V, Delhi, Motilal Banarsidass, 1990, p. 154.
6. F. Th. Stcherbatsky, *Buddhist Logic*, I, New York, Dover Publications, 1962, p. 459.
7. *Ibid.*, p. 465.
8. *Ibid.*, p. 465 f.
9. *Ibid.*, p. 461 f.
10. Matilal, *The Word and the World*, p. 37.
11. *Na jātiśabda bhedānām vācaka ānantyād* । *Buddhist Logic*, I, 461.
12. Diṇṇāga understands by the term *Vikalpa — Nāma, Jāti, Guṇa, Kriya, Dravya Kalpanā, Pramāṇa Samuccaya*, 1.3. Refer *Buddhist Logic*, II, 20.
13. *Buddhist Logic*, I, 471.
14. *Vākyapadīya*, III, Pt. I.14-15. *See* K.A.S. Iyer, *Bhartṛhari*, Poona, Deccan College, 1969, p. 209.
15. *Nyāya vartikā tātparyaṭikā* of Vācaspati Miśra, p. 486. *See* K.K. Raja, *Indian Theories of Meaning*, Adyar, The Adyar Library and Research Centre, 1963, p. 82.
16. B.K. Matilal, *Logic, Language and Reality*, Delhi, Motilal Banarsidass, 1985, p. 389.

8

Word-meaning and Sentence-meaning

Sentence-Holism versus Word-Atomism

ONE of the noteworthy features of Bhartṛhari's philosophy of language in his theory of *akhaṇḍapakṣa*. This theory stands for sentence-holism of a unique kind. According to it the sentence is the primary and indivisible unit of meaning. In the Part II of *Vākyapadīya*, he devotes full attention to the problem of sentence and sentence-meaning. He advances as many as eight main views regarding the nature of sentence-meaning. These theories offer us a glimpse of the complex nature of the problem. Bhartṛhari, in his inimitable style solves the problem, even at the cost of going against the prevalent and popular theories of his time. His concept of *akhaṇḍapakṣa* is a logical corollary of his communicative notion of language and meaning.

Bhartṛhari, himself, notes that basically there are two approaches to the problem of sentence and sentence-meaning. The first one is the indivisibility thesis (*akhaṇḍapakṣa*) and the latter one is the divisibility thesis (*khaṇḍapakṣa*). Following Matilal we can also call the former, 'sentence-holism' and the latter 'atomism'. The *Mīmāṁsakas* advocated the latter view and Bhartṛhari advocated the former view. As most of the Indian philosophical Systems, more or less, admit the communicative role of language, they raise the significant question — "how does the hearer cognises the whole 'sense', that a sentence conveys ?" According to Bhartṛhari sentence is indivisible whole and sentence-meaning is grasped as a whole. No doubt, we use several words in a sentence. But the words and word-meanings have no independent status in the communication of meaning through sentences. We can, of course, abstract words from a sentence, analyse them and examine them. But such abstractions are necessary for the study of linguistics and grammar. Isolated words and meanings are useful for such studies (*śāstra vyavahāra*).[1] But they are not fit for worldly transactions or communication (*loka vyavahāra*).[2] A sentence is not a compound-whole of words. Similarly sentence-meaning cannot be grasped by a computation word-meaning individually considered. The atomistic or *khaṇḍapakṣa* theorists, on the other hand, argue that word-meanings are not totally subservient to sentence-meaning. They have a sort of independence. The *Mīmāṁsā* theory of *khaṇḍapakṣa* has been interpreted in two ways by its two sub-schools. However, both the schools agree that a sentence is a composite entity constituted of words. These constitutive elements (words) are connected to make the 'whole' of the sentence. But regarding the question, how these constitutive elements are connected to produce the sentence-meaning, there is a difference of opinion. It is not a question of how the speaker connects them, but of how the hearers grasps the whole meaning from the separate units of word-meanings. Does he cognise the word-meanings separately and later on grasps them as conveying an unitary sense ? The *Bhaṭṭa* school of *Mīmāṁsā* says that the hearer understands the individual word-meanings first, and then joins them together to get the complete sentence-meaning. They are like separate railway coaches joined by couplings. But Prabhākara says that the hearer cognises the whole sentence by hearing simply the word-meanings in the context of the whole sentence. The first theory is called *abhihitānvaya vāda* and the latter theory *anvitabhidhāna vāda*.

According to the first theory, propagated by *Bhāṭṭa*, the hearer while listening to an utterance concentrates on individual word-meanings. But Prabhākara believes that the hearer grasps the whole meaning directly and deciphers the word-meaning in the context of a sentence. By implication it follows that for *Bhāṭṭa* sentence-meaning cannot mean anything more than the summing up of the word-meanings. On the other hand, for Prabhākara the sentence-meaning may be something more than the joining together of word-meanings. For him word-meanings, though independent, are not context-free. We also learn the meaning of a word only with reference to the sentence in which it occurs. Prabhākara's view may seem closer to Bhartṛhari's theory of *akhaṇḍapakṣa*, but it is not so. The question for Bhartṛhari is not simply the question of how we learn language or what is the actual process of hearer's understanding of the sentence-whole. His theory goes deeper than this. He considers the whole issue from the standpoint of his general philosophy of language.

Bhartṛhari's Argument for Sentence-Holism

At this stage a crucial question can be raised. I have claimed that most of the schools of Indian Philosophy envisage language as communicative and most of them put emphasis on hearer's meaning. Then why does Bhartṛhari adopt a totally different stand regarding the problem of sentence-meaning? He could have accepted anyone of these *khaṇḍapakṣa* theories, which were more popular. There are, of course, sufficient reason for Bhartṛhari to go against the current. Bhartṛhari himself offers a series of arguments in support of his unique stand. Before I examine these arguments, I will like to indicate some important facts which led Bhartṛhari to adopt sentence-holism. Bhartṛhari's explication of the communicative process of linguistic expression is radically different from other theories prevalent in Indian philosophical systems. For Bhartṛhari *vāk* is not just "uttered and articulated speech". It is a multi-layered phenomenon, and uttered speech (*vaikhārī*) is the final stage of the externalisation of the linguistic process. Before the speaker expresses himself audibly through uttered speech, he has to think of the appropriate words, and the meanings they are supposed to convey. Otherwise his utterances will be chaotic and in some cases mechanical. So *vaikhārī* (uttered) *vāk*, presupposes a mental and pre-utterance level, i.e., *madhyamā vāk*. This, in turn, further points to a level of unity. It is the level of unitary linguistic potentiality in which the series of words and their meanings are not discernible. This is the level of *paśyantī vāk*. The potent stage of verbalisability is thus, manifested in the form of particularised thought and intention. This, in turn, is externalised in the form of particular utterances. This way of explicating the speaker's way of communicating meaning implies that the uttered level along with its particularities and differentiations actually reflects the unity of thought and meaning. Whenever the speaker says something he expresses a 'sense' or a 'thought'. This sense or thought is one and unitary. For example, 'S' intends to express that he is hungry, so he would utter "I am hungry". Here the sentence contains three words, yet the 'intention' or what the speaker means, is unitary in nature. So for communicative purposes the unitariness of sentence-meaning has to be assumed by the speaker. Though he has to express what he intends to say through a series of words, yet the 'sense' expressed has a unity. Therefore, there is no implausibility in Bhartṛhari's claim that sentence and sentence-meaning are primary and an undifferentiated whole.

Again, if we look at the problem from the hearer's angle we are likely to understand the soundness of Bhartṛhari's claim. Hearer's understanding (*śābdabodha*) implies the grasping of a 'structured thought'. It is another way of saying that what he understands is the unitary sense expressed by the speaker. It is not a fragmented or piece by piece understanding. It cannot be denied that the hearer listens to the speaker's utterance in a sequential order, i.e., syllable by syllable. But he understands the unitary meaning by his inherent linguistic disposition (*pratibhā*). It is the power of understanding the meaning as a unitary whole. Hearer does not go on computing isolated words spoken by the utterer to understand the import of what is conveyed to him. In short, communication implies transference of a 'sense', 'idea' or 'thought'. And this can be possible if sentences, not the words, are taken to be the primary units of meaning.

We have examined the logical grounds of *akhaṇḍapakṣa* theory. Now let us see how Bhartṛhari defends his theory against his opponents. Bhartṛhari argues that if for the hearer's understanding, the sentential form of presentation is required, then why should we put unnecessary emphasis on the word-meanings. Most often word-meanings do not retain their individuality when fitted into a sentence. For example, the sentence *vṛkṣo-nāsti* (the tree, there is not) has two individual word-meanings. The meaning of the word 'tree' implies an existent object. But when we utter the second word *nāsti* (is not there), the first individual word implying 'existence' is cancelled by the second word. In such a case self-contradiction results, if the word-meanings are said to be independent, and a sentence is conceived as a conjunction of individual word-meanings. (*Vāk.*, II.241). Therefore, sentence-meaning is something more than concatenation of word-meanings, for there is a certain completeness and unitariness about sentence-meaning. Though sentence-meaning is presented through individual words, they do not have any autonomy in the matters of communication of meaning. Bhartṛhari says: "just as the senses which have each their essential field of operation, cannot perform the function without the body. In the same way individual words though expressive of their own meaning, have no meaning at all if they are isolated from the sentence". (*Vāk.*, II.419, 420).

However, it may be argued (as Bhartṛhari himself points out)[3] that sometimes the hearer may understand the whole sentence excepting just one word. In such cases the understanding of meaning of that particular word is helpful in making the cognition of the sentence complete. This proves that word-meanings are not totally statusless. For example, a man living in a city may not understand the import of the sentence, "bring a cuckoo from the forest", for he does not know what a 'cuckoo' means. In such a case it may be claimed that clarification of the meaning of one word 'cuckoo' would make the understanding of the sentence complete. Therefore, sentence-meaning is not self-complete, it is rather the word-meanings, which independently contribute to the completeness of sentence-meaning. But Bhartṛhari rejects this claim. According to him such confusions may arise due to the similarity of grammatical forms among some sentences. The sentence "bring a cuckoo from the forest" has a structural similarity with the sentence "bring fire-wood from the forest". This sort of similarity misleads us into thinking that the man who does not understand the word 'cuckoo' has actually grasped the rest of the meaning, "bring a '. . . .' from the forest". But Bhartṛhari argues that the commonness of grammatical form does not imply that the sentences have certain commonness of meaning. The import of the first sentence is totally different from the second one. There is nothing as the 'so-called' common-part. It is wrong on our part to conceive that the two sentence have similarity of meaning-components excepting one replaceable word, ('cuckoo' in place of 'fire-wood'). They are two independent sentences having two different sorts of implication. One does not bring a cuckoo in the same way as one brings the fire-wood.

> Just as one indivisible cognition appears to resemble another indivisible cognition in one part and to differ in another part, in the same way, even though the two sentences are indivisible and differ from each other

> completely, one perceives resemblane and difference between them in parts. The point may be illustrated by taking two pictures, the colour of one is green-blue while that of the other is green-yellow. The two would resemble each other partly and differ from each other partly. But in reality, they are two partless wholes. Similarly, two sentences which appear to resemble each other in having common words are really indivisible wholes.[4]

We may try to provide some more clear-cut examples to prove Bhartṛhari's point. "The coin is real" and "the time is real" — these two sentences have similar structure. But in the first case 'real' means 'not a counterfeit' and in latter case the term 'real' means something quite different. On the basis of the structural and grammatical similarity if one tries to interpret both the sentences as having similar import, then he is definitely misguided. It is the sentence-context and situation-context which determines the meanings of abstracted words.

Regarding the misconception that the knowledge of constitutent word-meaning is a surer path of the knowledge of the sentence-meaning, John Brough offers a very fitting example. By this he tries to prove Bhartṛhari's point. He states:

> We are apt to say from time to time, when struggling with a difficult passage in a foreign text, that we know all the words, but the meaning of the sentence escapes us. This however is a delusion. In such circumstances we are presumably attributing to one or more words a "meaning" which has not been extracted from this particular context, and the obvious comment is that we do not know all the words, since our knowledge does not include the manner of their occurrence in the context in question. In practice, of course, a more general, if vague, or of a meaning extracted from **similar** contexts frequently gives us sufficient clue; but this leads us in the first place to an understanding of the meaning of the sentence as a whole, and only afterwards, by an analysis of this understanding, to the attribution of meaning to the individual words.[5]

From the question of ambiguity one word in a sentence, let us now move to the problem of 'one-word' sentences. We often notice that sometimes the hearer can grasp the whole meaning, even if the speaker utters a single word or a phrase. A panic-stricken single word 'fire' can convey to the hearer that there is fire somewhere in the house. If the sentence-meaning is a conjunction of several word-meanings then such 'one-word' sentences are impossible. Here, by one-word sentence-meaning, we mean the completeness of what is to be conveyed or understood, achieved through the utterance of one word. Some schools of Indian philosophy believe that such completeness of meaning is possible because the hearer mentally supplies the words expressive of it. For example, when the hearer listens the single word 'fire', he mentally completes the sentence by inserting the words "The house is on —". Bhartṛhari does not subscribe to this view. The word actually uttered cannot bring the words unuttered to the mind. Rather when a single word is uttered, be it a noun or verb, it conveys the total meaning to the hearer without intervention of mental ordering of missing words. In such cases fitting in of the missing words do not supply the meaning. It is the context which is of more help in the grasping of the whole meaning.[6] Completeness of meaning is the test of a sentence. Therefore a single word can afford to have the significance of a sentence-meaning.

Bhartṛhari further clarifies this conception of 'completeness'. Incompleteness is more in the saying of a thing, rather than in the thing itself. There can be many instances when the word-meanings literally mean something, but imply something else. I have already discussed about Bhartṛhari's distinction between literal meaning, and implied or intended meaning. I need not repeat those examples. Let us take an example from our day-to-day experience. We often come across sentences which literally means praising somebody. But such sentences contain an element of sarcasm. When a boss reproaches his insincere employee by saying 'Ah, here comes the most sincere worker', it implies that he hints at his employee's insincerity. If the employee does not understand this intended sense, then the boss has failed to communicate his intention. This distinction between the literal meaning and intended meaning of a sentence very clearly proves that isolated word-meanings cannot be taken as the basis of sentence-meaning.[7] It is the sentence-meaning and the sentences, which are the primary units of linguistic communication.

These are some of the grounds on which Bhartṛhari rejects the primacy of word-meaning. What Bhartṛhari tries to establish is that sentences and sentence-meanings are indivisible and primary units, and they alone are real (*satya*). The individual words and their meanings have neither definiteness nor reality. In case of communication through language the speaker and the hearer have to operate with this factor of **unity**, which is achievable by sentence only. By saying that word-meanings are non-real, Bhartṛhari does not exactly denigrate the role of words. Bhartṛhari as a Grammarian, cannot afford to indulge in such a contradiction. He talks of reality of sentence-meaning in the context of linguistic communication. We neither express ourselves nor understand what is spoken to us through a series of meaning-units. "After a sentence has been understood we may look back at it, analyse it into words and maintain that we discern words in it. But if we do so during the course of the utterance itself, we are apt to lose the meaning of the sentence".[8] In essence, Bhartṛhari intends to make a distinction between language-in-use and 'language' as a subject-matter of the study of grammar and linguistics. As Brough very rightly points out:

> Bhartṛhari's view is simply that words and 'word-meanings' belong to the latter sphere. They constitute apparatus (not necessarily adequate) for the description of language events, but (roughly speaking) do not themselves 'exist' in the events described.[9]

Bhartṛhari's theory of *akhaṇḍapakṣa* has no parallel in Indian philosophy of language. As a result, we note that the concept of sentence-meaning has been analysed and explained in a totally different way by other philosophers of language. The *pada vādins* or the 'atomists', do not want to do away with the autonomy of words and word-meanings. So their main concern is to analyse the basic conditions of sentence-meaning. These conditions are presumed to give a completeness and unity to sentence-meaning. The three main conditions incorporated are *ākānkṣā, yogyatā*, and *sannidhi*. The *ākānkṣā* stands for syntactical completeness, whereas, *yogyatā* and *sannidhi* stand for semantical competence and phonetic continguity. But Bhartṛhari has no need for assuming such conditions as he considers sentence-meaning as a self-complete and non-divisible unit. The later *Nyāya* adds *tātparya* as the fourth condition. But *tātparya* refers more to the extra-linguistic contextual elements than to the proper linguistic elements. This condition is specifically meant for deciphering the contextual meaning with reference to the sentence as a whole. But it is never treated as a factor contributing to the completeness of sentence-meaning.

With this divergent attitude to the concept of sentence-meaning, it is natural for us to expect arguments and counter-arguments in support of each theory. Any book on Indian theories of language and meaning can provide us with a detailed account of such debates.[10] Especially, the opponents' argument figures most prominently, because *khaṇḍapakṣa* or atomism of word-meaning theory was most popular and well acknowledged theory of that time. Therefore, I will like to shift to a brief discussion on the modern way of handling the debate over the issue.

Two Opposing Modern Views on the Problem

The twentieth century theories of language and meaning initially were dominated by the Referential model. As a result the word meaning was considered to be primary. The Referential theory demands that words be directly connected with referents. So it is believed that a satisfactory theory of meaning must provide an account of how the meaning of a sentence depends upon the meaning of words. The popularity of the theory gets its support from one of the most perplexing feature of linguistic usage, i.e., how do we manage to express unlimited number of sentences out of the limited vocabulary ? The problem is sought to be resolved by assuming that our knowledge of word-meanings allows us to formulate varied sorts of sentences with the help of such word materials. Therefore without the knowledge of word-meanings, sentence-meanings are not decipherable. Some modern thinkers on Indian philosophy also present similar arguments in support of word-meaning primacy. But this view is not without flaws. Bhartṛhari's answer to such an argument would be that this perplexing feature of language does not necessarily imply the primacy of word-meaning. The isolated word-meanings do not lead us to the grasping as well as interpretation of sentence-meaning unless and until we know how the words are used in the particular context. The sum of word-meanings is not equivalent to a sentence-meaning. We can use the words in innumerable ways, not because we know the meanings of each word in the vocabulary, but because we have an inherent linguistic latency (*śabda-bhāvanā*) to use language in innumerable ways. By that he does not mean that knowledge of word-meanings is of no help in linguistic expressibility. There are sciences like grammar and lexicography which concentrate on words and word-meanings, and also on the valid rules of the ordering of the words in linguistic expression. What Bhartṛhari would like to vindicate is that in our analysis of communicative process, we have to assume that sentence-meaning is presented as a one and whole. And it is also understood by the hearer as one and whole. Donald Davidson in his famous paper "Truth and Meaning", seems to echo a similar argument. He says, "knowledge of the structural characteristics that make for meaningfulness in a sentence, plus knowledge of the meanings of the ultimate parts, does not add up to the knowledge of what a sentence means". But the reasons for his supporting the above view is in no way the same as that of Bhartṛhari's. Davidson is in search of a holistic theory of sentence-meaning in terms semantical theory of truth.[11] We shall come to Davidson's theory a little later. Full credit must be given to Frege who made a clear distinction between 'sense' and 'referent'. According to him the sentences express a 'thought' and the meanings of sentences are dependent on the 'sense' they represent. So he said that "only in the context of a sentence does a word have meaning". It was later Wittgenstein, who presented this thesis in another way by saying that words have meanings in the context of their *use* in language. Thereby he wanted to move away from the idea that our talk of the meaning of words must always be hooked to a referent. The 'Use theory' of meaning, is largely responsible in creating an awareness about the primacy of sentence and sentence-meaning. But his theory, in no way can be compared to Bhartṛhari's sentence-holism. For Bhartṛhari sentence is an undifferentiated whole. But Wittgenstein envisages that words get their significance only in the context of their use in a sentence. The autonomy of word-meaning in a sentence-context is not totally denied. So Wittgenstein's theory is rather akin to *Anvitabhidhāna vāda* of Prabhākara. Both the theories are very broadly speaking, sentence-contextual in nature. The concept of sentence-contextuality is almost unanimously accepted by subsequent philosophers. The central issue of sentence-context principle is, how do the words contribute to the meaning of a sentence ? Regarding this issue modern philosophers of language have broadly taken two different stands. Davidson and others analyse the problem from the standpoint of semantics, whereas Grice and his followers put emphasis on pragmatics of meaning.

To offer an account of how sentence acquires its meaning, another crucial question is brought in, i.e., what is the general character of those rules which in some sense must be mastered by anyone who speaks and understands a given sentence ? Donald Davidson offers an answer to the question which rests on the notion of truth-conditions. According to him an adquate account of meaning-rules for a language L, will show how the meanings of a sentence depend on meanings of words in L. Therefore a theory of meaning in any L, can be adequate if it contains a recursive definition of truth-in-L. In other words, in any language L, meaning of each element consists in what these elements (words or syntactical parts) contribute to truth-conditions of a sentence that contain it. According to him the relation between the definition of truth and the concept of meaning is as follows: "the definition works by giving the necessary and sufficient conditions for the truth of every sentence, and to give truth-condition is a way of giving the meaning of a sentence. To know the semantic concept of truth for a language is to know what it is for a sentence — any sentence — to be true, and this amounts, in one good sense we can give to the phrase, to understanding the language".[12] He adopts Tarski's notion of semantic truth to give a general picture of understanding meaning in any language. However, in the same paper he admits the inadequacy of the theory in handling many types of sentences which are not convertible into truth-condition principles. Those who believe in the supremacy of semantic notion of meaning, more or less, agree with Davidson, but they suggest some modifications here or there. I do not want to go into details of Davidson's very valuable paper, as our concern is limited to the question of sentence-meaning.

Grice and his followers on the other hand move in another direction. They are hard-core Communication-intention theorists, and believe that we do not need any general semantic rules for the communication of meaning. They locate all facts about the communicative intentions and beliefs of language users, and regularities concerning them, in pragmatics, not in semantics. What a sentence means is always relative to language. And language is an abstractly defined function. So all the dimensions of language cannot be caught within the framework of semantical definitions. Grice would contest Davidson's way of defining meaning by pointing out that he ignores the fact that most of our linguistic behaviour is conversational. No conversational behaviour would happily respond to such generalisations. So the contention of Grice and Schiffer is as follows: the speaker's meaning can be identified with what he is intending, in a certain way, to activate in his hearer a certain belief or action. The communicative meaning does not presuppose anything conventional or linguistic. Hence, **linguistic** meaning can be explained in terms of conventions over such intentions. The subsequent notions of referring and illocutionary forces are similarly non-conventional in their definition. Some philosophers view Grice's notion of speaker's 'intention' and 'intended meaning' as psychological. In case of lingustic or literal meaning he accepts the importance of convention. Therefore, it is presumed that he connects the semantics and the psychological elements of communication with the aid of practice and convention.[13]

I have given a brief outline of two opposing views regarding the nature of sentence-meaning. It can be summed up further as follows: one group of philosophers conceive sentence-meaning in terms of truth-conditions contributed by each element in a sentence; the other group does not bother about syntactical or linguistic elements nor about their truth-conditions. For them the communication of intended meaning of the speaker by an utterance, is all that matters. The debate that ensues from these two diverse outlook is still alive and hot.[14]

I do not want to fit in any of the above theory in Bhartṛhari's model. Bhartṛhari, no doubt, understands meaning in terms of communication. But he does not identify meaning with the speaker's intention or the hearer's understanding. In such an ancient theory it is futile to seek for the distinctive elements of semantical and psychological notions of language. Nor can we discern very clearly the elements of pragmatics and semantics in his theory of meaning. The problem of 'truth' does not figure at all in his theory of meaning, because he considers the 'referents' as belonging to the realm of 'linguistic constructs'. He is not also very much bothered about the varied uses of language, as all of them are parts of the meaning communicated. At trans-verbal level he considers the linguistic potency to be one whole, and each sentence represents a part of that whole.

References

1. K.A.S. Iyer, *Bhartṛhari,* p. 183.
2. *Ibid.*
3. The objection is raised by Bhartṛhari in *V.P.*, II. 74 & answered in *V.P.*, II. 94.
4. Iyer, *Bhartṛhari,* p. 195. Refer. *V.P.,* II. 93-94.
5. John Brough "Some Theories of Meaning", In *A Reader on the Sanskrit Grammarians,* p. 419.
6. Iyer, *Bhartṛhari,* 198, Refer. *V.P.,* II. 336 and Punyaraja's commentary on the verse.
7. *Vāk.*, 247.

   śtutinindā pradhaneṣu vākyesvartho ṇa tādṛśaḥ ।

   padānām pratibhāgena yādṛsaḥ parikalpyate ॥

   See Pillai - for trans.
8. Brough, "Some Indian Theories of Meaning", p. 417.
9. *Ibid.*
10. B.K. Matilal, *The Word and the World,* Chapter X, for a critical exposition of *Khaṇḍapakṣa* theories.
11. Donald Davidson, *Truth and Meaning.* Synthese XVII, (1967).
12. *Ibid.*, p. 310 — Davidson's theory is a complex one, I have provided a very Sketchy version of it, keeping in view our central issue, i.e., the notion of sentence-meaning.
13. Grice, "Meaning", In *Philosophical Review,* LXVI (1957), and "Utterer's Meaning, Sentence-Meaning and word-Meaning", In *Foundations of Language,* IV (1968). Also *see* Stephen R. Schiffer, *Meaning,* Clarendon Press, Oxford, 1972.
14. *Truth and Meaning: Essays on Semantics,* ed. by G. Evans and J. Mc-Dowell, Clarendon Press, Oxford, 1976. Please *see* the 'Introduction' and 'Two Theories of Meaning' by Brian Loar.

9

The Knowable and the Sayable

Bhartṛhari on What can be said

A SURVEY of Bhartṛhari's philosophy of language makes it clear that there is no end to what we can do with words (if not words then, atleast, word-potency). We think with words, conceive with words, carry on all sorts of conscious activities with words, including the act of communication. There is no limit to linguistic proliferation. Whatever is knowable is sayable and *vice-versa*. But is this sort of Pan-verbalism tenable as a theory ? Can we talk of any concept, including the concept of word or language without drawing its limits ? Does the concept of word or language defy all possibility of a structural boundary ? Bhartṛhari should have some answer for such vital questions about word itself. Here, in concluding my discussion on Bhartṛhari, I try to seek answer to such questions, which no philosoper of language can avoid.

To get the answer we must first of all be aware of the subtle distinction between the analysis of language-in-use, (the act of language) and the notion of language as a concept. In other words it is a distinction between what can be said **about** language and what can be said **in** language. I feel Bhartṛhari implicitly maintains this distinction in his philosophy of language. He mostly concentrates on the notion of language-in-use or what can be said **in** language. But while doing so he leads us very carefully to the structural bounds of language. At both the levels he maintains a Holistic stand.

When Bhartṛhari analyses the nature of language as a communicative act he leaves no aspect of it untouched. It is an accepted fact that we communicate with language. But it is not a simple matter of verbalisation. To talk we must think, we must experience, and we must discriminate. When somebody talks without thinking we call it an incoherent talk. Similarly when we listen to a tape-recorded talk we do not say the tape-recorder is talking. We say somebody's talk has been recorded. When we say a computer out of nowhere produces a sentence, we do not mean that the computer is writing. We say that a computer is programmed to produce such and such set of languages. In short, a thinking being can verbalise or atleast has the potentcy for verbalisation. A machine cannot think so it cannot talk in the sense man can talk in infinite number of ways with a limited vocabulary at his disposal. That is why Bhartṛhari includes in his analysis of language-in-use the concepts of 'thought', 'cognition' and 'ideas'. In such cases he is not indulging in a psychological analysis of the processes of awareness and thought. Rather he says that our explication of the verbal level of language remains incomplete without bringing in the concepts of 'thought', 'awareness' and 'cognition'. We cannot understand how we do things with words just by keeping ourselves within the narrow confines of actual linguistic utterance. To do so is to indulge in a form of linguistic behaviourism. Even later Wittgenstein who disposes of such mental concepts as 'understanding' and 'thinking' as misnomer has admitted this, for he says :

> "If a lion could talk we could not understand him".
> (*P.I.*, p. 223)

Why does he say so ? Simply because the lion does not intend to communicate, nor is he aware of what he is saying. Lion's talking is not an expression of his thought and experience. Therefore according to Wittgenstein, "...speaking is a part of activity or a form of life". The 'form of life', Wittgenstein often talks of in his *Philosophical Investigations*, will turn into a routine running of the machine, if it does not include man's experience, thought and consciousness. We always express a chunk of our experience, knowledge, emotion etc. through verbal expressions. This is why Bhartṛhari does not hesitate to talk of connecting language-in-use with the mental level. Of course, his time and cultural background did not allow him to be a captive of the craze for specialisation.

There is no watertight distinction between the philosophy of mind and the philosophy of language, between psychology and epistemology, in Bhartṛhari's philosophy. Therefore, with equal ease, he points out that not only language needs thought, but thought needs language. He very rightly points out that thought in any form, be it cognition or awareness, needs conceptualisation. And conceptualisation, in turn, needs word-loadedness. Conceptualisation implies discrimination and assimilation, and this is done through words. He offers a comprehensive account of knower, known and knowledge; and consciousness, referent and linguistic usage. For, all of them are bound by word-interpenetrability. As long as we are thinking and talking about phenomenal world or the experiences of our life there is no epistemic gap between the thought, language and referent. Understood in this sense, Bhartṛhari's position can be summed up as, whatever is **knowable** is **sayable**, and whatever is **sayable** is **knowable**.

Coming down to the level of utterances Bhartṛhari seems to exhibit the same trend of Holism and comprehensiveness of attitude. For him language is not primarily meant for reporting facts or states-of-affair. Indian thought, as such, shows no partiality towards assertions and factual statements. Excepting *Nyāya*, which adheres to a Realistic world-view, for other systems there is no clear-cut epistemic gulf between independent objective reality and consciousness. Especially in case of *śabda* as a method of knowledge, it has always been insisted that such knowledge acquired through language is not primarily about facts. It is conceived as a method of acquiring knowledge about non-factual things like morality, injunctions or philosophical speculations. The question of factual knowledge is left to the methods of *pratyakṣa* (perception) *anumāna* (inference), etc. In case of *śabda pramāṇa* 'truth' is not the central point, rather 'validity' occupies the key-position. So 'truth' is not exclusively the defining characteristic of *pramā*, whereas in Western epistemology knowledge means 'truth'. It is a contradiction in terms to say, "I know but it is false". For Bhartṛhari, who primarily conceives *śabda* as the only basis of his philosophical analysis does not leave any scope for interpreting language exclusively in terms of factual knowledge. Language as an element of expressiveness is connected with multifarious dimensions of awareness and cognition, including the cognition of facts. We can linguistically express our thoughts about facts, as much as about religion, poetic emotions, *dharma* (moral principles including injunctions), metaphysical predilections, about the rules of grammar and many more things. Bhartṛhari never seems to bother about this element of multiple uses of language. He seems to take this important feature of language for granted. But in connection with explanation about some philosophical misconceptions about language he cites examples to show the difference of form. For example, to show that words and sentences need not primarily refer to existing facts he offers the example of *gandharva nagara* (celestial city), which may be used in fiction, poetry or in story-telling. Again he very meticulously shows that we can talk of time, space, existence, substance, in general sense as concepts, as well as in specific sense, when used in particular contexts. There are plenty of evidences where he analyses particular forms of sentential use to show the differences in their contextual meanings. But nowhere does he make any conscious effort to show that they are different 'language-games' (to borrow Wittgenstein's phase). As such in Indian philosophy of language, the plurality of linguistic structure has never been seriously challenged. Instead Indian philosophers, including Bhartṛhari, have been more bothered about the layers of meaning. So a rich and powerful discussion on the types of communicated meaning, such as primary meaning (*avidhā*), metaphorical meaning (*lakṣanā*), suggestive meaning (*vyañjanā*) etc., are carried on by most of the schools of Indian philosophy. But the issue of deciphering the meaning of different forms of language is left to hearer's mastery of language. "It is evening now" and "time is eternal" — these are two sentences of different forms about one concept, i.e., time. But Bhartṛhari would see no scope for confusion here. He would take it for granted that the speaker as well as the hearer (and for that matter anybody who has mastered a language) can know that the first sentence is about a particular time and the second is about 'time' as a general concept. In case of the first sentence the hearer may respond by looking at the sky, or hurrying back home. But in the latter case he is given a choice either to accept the conceptual scheme about time or reject it. Here there is no scope for linguistic misunderstanding or confusing the rules of one language-game with another. This easy acceptance of pluralistic language-view may be due to the fact that Bhartṛhari does not have a model oriented theory of meaning.

According to him 'meaning' means what is communicated by the speąker to the hearer. In this regard Bhartṛhari's attitude is clearly antagonistic to what Carnap has to say about the scope of meaningfulness.

> Many linguistic utterances are analogous to laughing in that they have only expressive function, no representative function. Examples of this are cries like 'oh', 'ah', on a higher level lyrical verses ... have only an expressive function. Metaphysical propositions are neither true nor false, because they assert nothing — But they are like, laughing, lyrics and music, expressive.[1]

Carnap in one sweep not only denigrates metaphysics to the level of laughing but also bundles up poetry, aesthetics, values, morality into meaningless emotive outbursts. To be meaningful is to assert and such assertions either have to be true or false. A straightforward version of this attitude can be noticed in Wittgenstein's remarks. He advises:

> To say nothing except what can be said, i.e. propositions of natural science.
>
> (*Tractatus,* 6. 53)

And,

> A proposition shows how things stand if it is true".
>
> (4.022)

Some Modern Views on the Problem

Both these versions of Referential model draw their line of **sayability** and **knowability** within the bounds of what fits into mould of truth-conditionality. A sentence is meaningful if and only if the speaker has the knowledge of the conditions under which it would be either true or false. One cannot fit in the sentences on religion, morality, poetics, political ideologies, grammatical rules and many more significant linguistic expressions within its scope. The modern philosophy of language and meaning is the typical product of a period which marked the triumph of natural science and death of metaphysics. So the fascination for natural sciences, along with its emphasis on truth and neatness of structure continued to guide the development of subsequent philosophy of language. One comes across the strong fascination for 'truth-conditions' and 'assertions' in subsequent theories of meaning. The central core of most of the philosophy of language is a theory of truth, and sometimes at the periphery lies a theory of 'force'. The types of 'force' that Austin and Searle enlists are more about various modes of assertions (either in the form of imperative, interrogative, promise statements, etc.), than modes of experience. By experience, I mean all sorts of it, which are co-extensive with life. Sometimes, these philosophers talk of Holism.[2] But it is not a Holism of Bhartṛhari's type. It is a limited sense of Holism, with reference to a particular theory of truth or a particular form of language. In this connection I deem it fit to quote some Indologists who are very frank about this mono-model adopted by modern philosophers of language. John Brough, the famous scholar on Bhartṛhari and Indian philosophy of grammar, puts it more explicitly :

> Most philosophic discussions of meaning confine themselves to a relatively small portion of language behaviour, namely, statements which describe or report a state of affairs — the propositions of the natural sciences, or, more generally, such statements as are traditionally handled by logic. This part of language possesses enormous importance and prestige, and is also the least difficult to deal with in a more or less clear fashion. But its treatment frequently suffers from a forgetfulness of the fact that propositions (or the formulae of symbolic logic) are nonetheless language; and I would suggest that a wider linguistic understanding is most desirable . . . logic, mathematics, linguistics, science in general, all convey their messages in language, and this language, however technical, **cannot be understood** save in a manner which is fundamentally similar to the understanding of everyday language. As the ancient Indian might say, the utterances of the costermonger, the language of the great poet, and the formulae of the atomic physicist are all in some sense manifestations of the same divine *vāk*.[3]

Harold Coward, another important scholar on Bhartṛhari is more cautions in his remarks. He says

> While not all may agree with Indian approach in general or with Bhartṛhari in particular, it is a view of language which makes sense of poetry, revealed scripture, science, the mystical chanting of *mantras*, and in addition, strongly resonates with our ordinary everyday experience of coffee-cup chat.[4]

Many Indologists like J.G. Arapura,[5] Frits Staal[6] and others are also very vociferous in their criticism of a form of reductionism adopted by modern philosophers which reduces language analysis into the model of scientific and factual referents. They admit the importance of the Holistic approach of Indian philosophy of language.

I referred to these views not to prove that all that the modern philosophers of language present, are of no value. I simply argue in favour of a comprehensive and holistic account of the language — a language that we use in our life. Without this, the philosophy of language would be alienated from the level of practice. The concept of 'language' is dynamic and a 'living' concept and it should not be robbed of its life by lifting it to the thin air of models and forms. As Wittgenstein who suggested a monomodel of language earlier, himself realises:

> Man possesses the ability to construct a language capable of expressing every sense, without having any idea how each word has meaning or what meaning is . . .
>
> Everyday language is a part of human organism and is no less complicated than it.
>
> (*Tractatus,* 4.002)

Later on a grand attempt was made by Wittgenstein first, in his *Philosophical Investigations,* and then in subsequent works, especially *Culture and Value* to breathe life into the philosophical study of language. Grice and his followers also contributed their mité to keep language within the bounds of its naturalness. I must refer here to Wittgenstein's contribution in a little detail to show that the obsession with factual language is not the whole of the story. In *Philosophical Investigations* Wittgenstein makes efforts to reveal the close relation between life and language. Language is presented here as a part of life. But to a large extent it turns out to be a negative way of analysis. He treats philosophers and their ontological commitments as muddled and confused in nature. But he is more forthright in his books, *Culture and Value* and *Philosophical Remarks*, etc. In these books we note that there is a conscious opposition to the intellectualists' categorisation of language and reality. He attempts to check the tendency to theorise or rationally build up theoretical superstructures. And by doing so he openly accepts the validity and significance of our linguistic expressions about values, aesthetics, religion, even mystical experiences. Grice, on the other hand believes that language is a matter of conversations and primarily a matter of communication of intention. They point towards a more comprehensive and holistic treatment of natural language. In future newer and better models of comprehensive and holistic theories of language are likely to emerge. I shall like to conclude this part of my discussion by quoting a very significant remark made by Strawson. He says :

> Nevertheless the actual use of linguistic expressions remains his (Philosopher's) sole and essential point of contact with the reality which he wishes to understand, conceptual reality: for this is the only point from which the actual mode of operation of concepts can be observed. If he severs this vital connection, all his ingenuity and imagination will not save him from lapses into the arid and absurd.[7]

Bhartṛhari on the Limiting Concepts of Knowability and Sayability

In the last section, I have deviated from the central theme of our discussion about the idea of **knowable** and **sayable**. But I feel such a deviation was necessary to prove that the limits of the knowability and sayability must not be bound by an artificial superstructure, however neat it may be. We have examined Bhartṛhari's views on what we can say **in** language; now let us dwell briefly on what his views are regarding what we can say **about** language. He explains the concept of linguistic communication with the help of two fundamental presuppositions. They are : (1) there is an inherent fitness in words to express meaning (*yogyatā*), and (2) there is an inherent ability to understand the meaning expressed through language (*pratibhā*). In a sense, both these concepts represent two dimensions of communication; the speaker's ability to convey meaning or thought and the hearer's ability to grasp the meaning. In case of both the concepts Bhartṛhari admits their ineffability. They can be presumed but they cannot be explained and defined. In other words they are neither **knowable** nor **sayable**.

(a) *Yogyatā*

Yogyatā is one of the basic presuppositions **about** the nature of language. Language implies the use of words with certain grammatical form and syntactical structure. But words are not themselves language. It is **language** because it expresses meaning. So words are endowed with the capacity to express meaning, and there is an inherent fitness in the words to express the meaning. This is called *yogyatā*. Therefore according to Bhartṛhari there is an internal and eternal relation between word and meaning. The relation between word and meaning is indicated by the use of genitive case ('Y is the meaning of X'). Though the relationship is the basis of communicative language, yet there is no expression to designate this relation as a **relation**. Therefore Bhartṛhari uses analogies like illumination and illuminator (*prakāśa* and *prakāśatva*) etc., to explain the nature of this relation.[8] The nature of '**Relation**', regarding relationship between word and meaning is not directly expressible. While stating this unique theory Bhartṛhari expects objections from his opponents. The opponents may raise a valid objection. If 'Relation' is inexpressible then one cannot even use the word 'inexpressible', because in saying so he has expressed something. Here Bhartṛhari's answer is very insightful and it directly hints at the paradoxes of linguistic presuppositions. He says, in stating "all that I am saying is false" (*sarvaṁ mithyā brabhimi*) "one does not intend to include that very sentence in the scope of its meaning, for then, as what one is saying would be implicitly false, the intended meaning would not be conveyed. Generally, what is expressive cannot at the same time be what it expresses, and if something X is conveyed by Y then Y cannot itself be expressed by something other than Y".[9] The argument reminds us of its Western counterpart, i.e., the, 'paradox of the liar'.

This interesting critique of the notion of signification relation between word and meaning has been discussed by H. Herzberger and R. Herzberger in detail,[10] They call it 'Bhartṛhari's paradox'. This Paradox is based on the general notion of the axiom about 'relation', i.e., non-relation can be its relata. The paradox that

Bhartṛhari presents can be justified on another ground also "An item is usually signified by a signifier, 'linguistic expression', on the basis of some property or aspect belonging to the signified object, but since characters or aspects of the signification relation (or relation in general) are completely exhausted by its two relata, it is completely colourless — in fact too colourless to be significant at all".[11]

> But there is no (proper) designator of the (said) relation that speaks of (or designates) it on the basis of its own feature (*dharma*). (For) due to its being totally undermined by others (its two relata), its own feature is not designated.
>
> (Verse III.3.4)[12]

Bhartṛhari argues that since the speaker, utters the designator (words) in order to convey the designated (the meaning), each utterance implicitly suggests that "this (word) **is** that (the meaning expressed)". So the relation is implicitly **shown**, but it cannot be **said**.

(b) *Pratibhā*

The other fundamental concept **about** linguistic communication is *Pratibhā*, the intuitive flash of understanding through which hearer grasps the meaning of expressed words. Of course, the term *pratibhā* has been used by Bhartṛhari with wider implications. I shall here, focus only on the concpet of *pratibhā* in relation to linguistic understanding. For him this intuitive capacity is different from the perçeptual and inferential ways of knowing. This is the means of understanding of the undifferentiated meaning of a sentence as a whole. But it implies something more than this. It is a knowledge of the meaning communicated, in which the sentence expressed through the sequential presentation of words, and the meaning implied, are merged into one. So sometimes it is identified with *śabda bhāvanā,* (linguistic latency). This unified principle is presupposed to explain the hearer's understanding, for, while understanding a sentence the hearer does not distinguish words from meanings. However, this principle of understanding, as such, is not definable. Bhartṛhari says, "This (*pratibhā*) cannot in any way be explained to others in terms such as "it is this"; its existence is ratified only in the individual's experience of it, and the experiencer himself cannot describe it" (*VP*, II.146).[13] This again shows that the structural concepts of language cannot be described in language. It is not **sayable**. And on the basis of Bhartṛhari's identification between the **knowable** and **sayable**, we can say that *pratibhā* is not also **knowable**. The limits of knowability and sayability gradually point to further limits which reflects Bhartṛhari's metaphysical position. Ultimately he shows that no language can say anything about the Reality, be it the linguistic reality or be it the reality of the phenomenal world. Our sentences are nothing more than the fragments and bits of meaning-whole. The principle of language as such, is not **sayable**, for whatever is sayable is only a part of the whole, that our mind selects for practical and worldly transactions. Similarly what the world **is** cannot be expressed, because we can at best explain a particular dimension of the objective world that we intend to know and talk about. We presuppose that the world **is** there, and the language **is** there, but these presuppositions themselves are not **sayable**. Whatever is **sayable** is finite and differentiated manifestation of the one *śabda tattva.*

Wittgenstein on the Limits of Sayability

But one last question remains: if all sorts of linguistic expressions are not real from the ultimate point of view, then why does Bhartṛhari labours to produce such a big treatise on the nature of language ? Does he conceive the entire programme of philosophical analysis the way Wittgenstein understands it in *Tractatus* ? Wittgenstein at the end of his book declares :

> My propositions serve as elucidation in the following way: anyone who understands me eventually recognizes them as non-sensical, when he has used them as steps to climb up beyond them. (He must, so to speak, throw away the ladder after he has climbed up it) He must transcend these propositions, then he will see the world alright.
>
> (*Tractatus,* 6.54)

But Bhartṛhari's programme as well as goal is totally different from Wittgenstein's *Tractatus.* Bhartṛhari would say that we need to know about the nature and functioning of language in order to transcend it to attain the knowledge of the ultimate Reality, i.e., *śabda Brahman.* He undertakes the programme of philosophical analysis of language to prove that everything is phenomenal, and is explainable only in terms of the principle of language. So the entire knowledge about the language-in-use can be thrown like a step once we have climbed it and achieved the knowledge of the *Brahman*. But for Wittgenstein the programme is meant for saving the philosophers from indulging in nonsense. We cannot and should not talk of things that are not factual in nature. Our statements about ethics, aesthetics, religion and metaphysics as well as the very nature of language lie beyond the scope of the **sayability**, for they do not talk of the world.

References

1. Carnap, *Philosophy and Logical Syntax,* London: R.K.P., 1935, p. 28.
2. Davidson, *Truth and Meaning.*
3. John Brough, "Some Indian Theories of Meaning", In *A Reader on the Sanskrit Grammarians,* p. 423.
4. Harold G. Coward, *The Sphoṭa Theory of Language,* Motilal Banarsidass, Delhi.
5. J.G. Arapura, "Some Perspectives on Indian Philosophy of Language", In *Revelation in Indian Thought.,* ed. by Coward and Sivaraman Dharma Publishing, 1977.
6. Frits Staal, 'The Concept of Metalanguage and its Indian Background", In *Journal of Indian Philosophy,* III (1975), p. 319.
7. P.F. Strawson, "Analysis, Science and Metaphysics", In *The Linguistic Turn,* ed. by R. Rorty, Chicago: Chicago University Press, 1967, p. 320.
8. *Vākyapadīya,* III. 3.3. — B.K. Matilal renders the translation of the verse in following manner: "This is the signifier (*Vācaka*) of that, and that is the signified (*Vācya*) of this. The thatness (*tattva*) of the connection between the word and what it means is thus understood from the genetive ending. Hence its own nature (that-ness) is designated.
9. *Vākyapadīya,* III.3.3-28 — translation taken from *Encyclopaedia of Indian Philosophies, V.P.,* 158.
10. H. Herzberger and R. Herzberger, "Bhartṛhari's Paradox", In *Journal of Indian Philosophy,* No. 9, 1981, pp. 3-32.
11. B.K. Matilal, *The Word and the World,* p. 130.
12. Translation rendered by B.K. Matilal, *Word and World,* p. 130.
13. Translation rendered by John Brough, "Indian Theories", p. 420.

Glossary of Sanskrit Terms

Adhyāsa	superimposition.
Āgama	scriptural truth or verbal means of knowledge.
Ahaṃkāra	ego.
Akhaṇḍapakṣa	the theory that believes that sentence is the primary unit of meaning.
Anumāna	inference.
Artha	word-meaning as distinct from the word-sound.
Ātman	self.
Avidyā	the obscuring veil of human ignorance that, when removed, reveals knowledge of reality.
Bhāṣya	commentary.
Brahman	the Absolute, the Reality.
Buddhi	the intellect or the level of consciousness characterised by intelligent discrimination.
Darśana	philosophical point of view or philosophical system.
Dhvani	the uttered syllables of a word.
Jñāna	knowledge or cognition.
Kalpanā	mental constructs.
Kāraṇa	cause.

Kārya	effect.
Krama	sequence.
Madyamā Vāk	language as thought that has not yet been uttered.
Maḥāvākyas	the great criterion sentences of the *Upanisaḍs*, e.g., "That thou art".
Manas	the mental organ that collects and co-ordinates informations.
Māyā	the illusion of the manifoldness of the world which is really the unitary Absolute or Brahman.
Mokṣa	liberation or release from the suffering and bondage of this world leading to identification with the Absolute.
Nāda	physical sound.
Paśyantī Vāk	the level of intuitive understanding of the sentence-meaning as whole non-verbal level of language.
Pramā	true cognition or knowledge.
Pramāṇa	valid methods of knowledge.
Pratibhā	the capacity to directly grasp the real meaning.
Pratyakṣa	perception.
Pratyaya	concept or idea.
Śabda	language as a general concept or the linguistic principle.
Śabda Brahman	language or linguistic principle as the ultimate Reality or the intertwined unity of word and consciousness that is the one and ultimate Reality according to Bhartṛhari.
Śabda Pramāṇa	the verbal method of knowledge.

Śabda Tattva	the word principle.
Śabda Bhāvanā	the linguistic potency inherent within conscious being.
Saṃskāra	a memory trace that has the dynamic quality of expressing itself.
Saṃketa	convention of language or linguistic convention.
Samjñā	definition, named.
Samjñin	definiendum, name.
Śāstra	authoritative teaching or analytical discourse about a particular branch of knowledge.
Sattā	existence.
Sphoṭa	meaning whole or linguistic potency that eternally exists within consciousness and which can be manifested by spoken words.
Śruti	primary scripture such as the *Vedas,* the *Brahmanas* and the *Upanisaḍs.*
Satkārya vāda	the theory that effect is pre-existent in cause.
Tātparya	contextual meaning.
Upacāra Sattā	metaphorical existence.
Vācya	signified, the meaning-content.
Vācaka	signifier, the words that express the meaning.
Vaikhārī Vāk	the level of uttered speech.
Vāk	language that is thought of as having various levels of manifestation, from the level of spoken word to the level of intuitive understanding of meaning.
Vākya	sentence.
Varṇa	letter sounds.

Vikalpa	linguistic construct.
Vṛtti	a commentary.
Vyākaraṇa	grammar, the grammar school — one of the traditional schools of Indian philosophy dealing with language and the linguistics.
Vyāvahārika	worldly usages or worldly affairs.
Yogyatā	logical compatibility in the context of word-meaning relation it means the inherent capacity of words to express meanings.

Selected Bibliography

Arapura, J.G., 'Some Perspectives on Indian Philosophy of Language', In *Revelation in Indian Thought*, ed. by H.G. Coward and Sivaraman, Dharma Publishing, 1977.

Austin, J., *How to Do Things with Words*, London : Oxford University Press, 1962.

Ayer, A.J., *Language Truth and Logic*, New York: Dover Press, 1946.

Bhartṛhari, *Vākyapadīya* I, ed. and trans. by K.A. Subramania Iyer, Poona : Deccan College, 1966.

———, *Vākyapadīya* II, K.A.S. Iyer, Delhi: Motilal Banarsidass, 1971.

———, *Vākyapadīya*, Iyer Part-III, Canto. II, 1974.

———, *Vākyapadīya*, Canto I and II, K.R. Pillai, Delhi: Motilal Banarsidass.

———, *Vākyapadīya*, S.N. Shukla (with commentary), Chowkhamba Sanskrit Series, 1961.

Bhattacharya, B.P., *A Study in Language and Meaning*, Calcutta : Progressive Publishers, 1962.

Bhattacharya, J.V., *Nyāya Mañjarī of Jayanta Bhaṭṭa*, Delhi: Motilal Banarsidass, 1965.

Bradley, F.H., *Principles of Logic*, Pts. I and II, London: Oxford University Press, 1922.

Brough, J., 'Some Indian Theories of Meaning' and 'Theories of General Linguistics of the Sanskrit Grammarians', In *A Reader on the Sanskrit Grammarians*, Delhi: Motilal Banarsidass, 1972.

Caradona, G., *Pāṇini : A Survey of Research,* The Hague : Mouten and Co., 1976.

Carnap, R., *Philosophy and Logical Syntax,* London : Routledge and Kegan Paul, 1935.

Chakravarti, *Linguistic Speculation of Hindus,* Calcutta : Calcutta University Press, 1983.

Coward, H.G., *Sphoṭa Theory of Language,* Delhi: Motilal Banarsidass, 1980.

Coward and K.K. Raja (eds.), *The Encyclopaedia of Indian Philosophies,* Vol. V, (The Philosophy of Grammarians), Motilal Banarsidass, 1990.

Cultural Heritage of India, Vol. I., Calcutta: The Ramakrishna Mission, 1982.

Davidson, D., 'Thought and Talk', In *Mind and Language,* ed. by S.D. Guttenplan, Oxford: Clarendon Press, 1975.

———, 'Truth and Meaning', *Synthese* XVIII, 1967.

Datta, D.M., *Six Ways of Knowing,* Calcutta: Calcutta University Press, 1972.

Daya Krishna, *Indian Philosophy : A Counter Perspective,* Delhi: Oxford University Press, 1991.

De., S.K. *Studies in the History of Indian Poetries,* London: Luzac and Co., 1925.

Evans, G. and Mc-Dowell, J., *Truth and Meaning : Essays on Semantics,* Oxford: Clarendon Press, 1976.

Frege, G., 'The Thought: A Logical Inquiry', In P.F. Strawson's *Philosophical Logic,* Oxford: Oxford University Press, 1977, pp. 17-38.

Grice, H.P., 'Meaning', In *Philosophical Review,* LXVI, 1957.

———, "Utterer's Meaning, Sentence Meaning and Word Meaning', In *Foundations of Language,* IV (1968).

Herzberger, H. and Herzberger, R., 'Bhartṛhari's Paradox', In *Journal of Indian Philosophy,* 67, 1970, pp. 145-67.

Iyer, K.A. Subramania., *Bhartṛhari,* Poona: Deccan College, 1969.

———, *Vākyapadīya: Some Problems*, Poona : Bhandarkar Oriental Research Institute, 1982.

Joshi, S.D., *The Sphoṭanirṇaya of Kaunda Bhaṭṭa*, Poona, 1976.

Keith, A.B., *A History of Sanskrit Literature*, Oxford : Oxford University Press, 1928.

Kunjunni Raja, K., *Indian Theories of Meaning*, Madras : Adyar Library, 1969.

Lewis, David., 'Languages and Language', In *Language Mind and Knowledge*, ed. by K. Gunderson, Minneapolis: University of Minnesota Press, 1975.

Locke, John, *Essays Concerning Human Understanding*, Book III, 1894.

Matilal, B.K., *Perception*, Delhi: Oxford University Press, 1986.

———, *The Word and the World*, Delhi: Oxford University Press, 1990.

———, *Language, Logic and Reality*, Delhi : Motilal Banarsidass, 1985.

McGinn, Collin, *The Character of Mind*, Oxford: Oxford University Press, 1982.

Misra, G., *Language, Reality and Analysis*, New York: E.J. Brill, 1991.

———, *Advaita Philosophy: Its Method, Scope and Limits*, Bhubaneswar, 1976.

Murti, T.R.V., *Studies in Indian Thought*, Delhi: Motilal Banarsidass, 1983.

Pāṇini, *Aṣṭādhyāyī and Padamañjarī of Haradatta*, ed. by D.D. Sastri and K.P. Shukla, *Bharati Series*, Varanasi, 1965-67.

Patañjali, *Vyākaraṇa Mahābhāṣya, Bombay Sanskrit Series*, ed. by F. Kielhorn, 1892.

Pandeya, R.C., *The Problem of Meaning in Indian Philosophy*, Delhi : Motilal Banarsidass, 1963.

Passmore, J., *Recent Philosohers : A Supplement to Hundred Years of Philosophy*, London: Duckworth, 1985.

Patnaik, T., 'Language, Thought and Communication — An Appraisal of Bhartṛhari's Theory of Language', In *Indian Philosophical Quarterly*, Vol. XV, No. 3, July 1988.

———, 'Some Reflections on Bhartṛhari's Notion of Sentence-Meaning', In *Visva Bharati Journal of Philosophy*, Vol. XXIV, No. 2, Vol. XXV Feb.-August, 1988. Published in 1989.

———, 'A Note on Bhartṛhari's Theory of *Sphoṭa*', In *Prajñā*, Utkal Journal of Philosophy, Vol. XI, March 1990.

———, 'Intention and Convention in Communication—Reunderstanding Bhartṛhari', In *Indian Philosophical Quarterly*, Vol. XIX, No. 4, October 1992.

———, 'The Word and the World — Bhartṛhari and Diṇṇāga', In *Visva Bharati Journal of Philosophy*, XXVIII, No.2, Feb. 1992.

———, 'The Problem of Intention in Bhartṛhari's Philosophy of Language', In *Prajñā*, Vol. XII, March 1990.

Pitcher, G., *The Philosophy of Wittgenstein*, Prentice Hall, 1964.

Quine, W.V., *Word and Object*, Cambridge : Mass., Technology Press, 1960.

———, *From a Logical Point of View*, Harvard University Press, 1953.

Radhakrishnan, S., *Indian Philosophy*, Vols. I and II, London: George Allen and Unwin, 1962.

Ryle, G., *Collected Papers* II, London : Hutchinson and Co. Ltd., 1973.

Śaṅkara, *Brahma Sūtra-bhāṣya.*

Sastri, G., *A Study in Dialectics of Sphoṭa*, Delhi : Motilal Banarsidass, 1980.

———, *The Philosophy of Word and Meaning*, Calcutta : Sanskrit College, 1959.

Searle, J., *Speech Acts: An Essay in Philosophy of Language*, Cambridge: Cambridge University Press, 1969.

Sellars, W., 'Conceptual Change', In *Conceptual Change*, ed. by D. Pearce and P. Maynard, Dordrecht, 1973.

Stace, W.T., *A Critical History of Greek Philosophy*, Macmillan, 1982.

Stall, F., 'Sanskrit Philosophy of Language', In *Current Trends in Linguistics*, Vol. V, ed. by T.A. Sebeok *et al.*, The Hague, 1969, 46-94.

———, 'The Concept of Meta-Language and Its Background', In *Journal of Indian Philosophy*, III, 1975.

———, *A Reader on the Sanskrit Grammarians*, Delhi: Motilal Banarsidass, 1972.

Stcherbatsky, F. Th., *Buddhist Logic*, New York: Dover Publications, 1962.

Strawson, P.F., *Logico-Linguistic Papers*, London, Methuen and Co., 1974.

———, *Analysis and Metaphysics*, Oxford: Oxford University Press, 1992.

Tarski, A., 'The Semantical Conception of Truth', In *Philosophy and Phenomenological Research*, 1944.

Wittgenstein. L., *Tractatus Logico-Philosophicus*, Routledge and Kegan and Paul, 1974.

———, *Philosophical Investigations*, London: Basil and Blackwell, 1978.

———, *Blue and Brown Books*, London: Basil and Blackwell, 1958.

———, *Culture and Value*, Oxford: Basil and Blackwell, 1980.

Index